Carving Wildfowl Canes and Walking Sticks with Power

FRANK C. RUSSELL

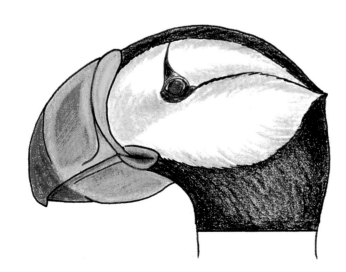

880 Lower Valley Road, Atglen, PA 19310 USA

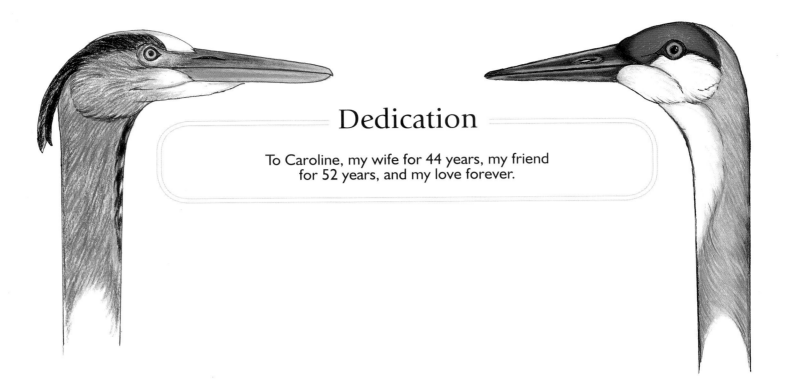

Dedication

To Caroline, my wife for 44 years, my friend
for 52 years, and my love forever.

Designed by John P. Cheek
Cover design by Bruce M. Waters
Type set in Giovanni Book/Humanist 521 BT

ISBN: 978-0-7643-1589-3
Printed in China

Schiffer Books are available at special discounts for bulk purchases for sales promotions or premiums. Special editions, including personalized covers, corporate imprints, and excerpts can be created in large quantities for special needs. For more information contact the publisher:

Published by Schiffer Publishing Ltd.
4880 Lower Valley Road
Atglen, PA 19310
Phone: (610) 593-1777; Fax: (610) 593-2002
E-mail: Info@schifferbooks.com

For the largest selection of fine reference books on this and related subjects,
please visit our website at: **www.schifferbooks.com**
We are always looking for people to write books on new and related subjects.
If you have an idea for a book please contact us at the above address.

This book may be purchased from the publisher.
Include $5.00 for shipping.
Please try your bookstore first.
You may write for a free catalog.

In Europe, Schiffer books are distributed by
Bushwood Books
6 Marksbury Ave.
Kew Gardens
Surrey TW9 4JF England
Phone: 44 (0) 20 8392 8585; Fax: 44 (0) 20 8392 9876
E-mail: info@bushwoodbooks.co.uk
Website: www.bushwoodbooks.co.uk

Contents

Foreword

I hope you enjoy the cane and walking stick head and handle patterns I have presented in this book. Primary attention has been given to carving the decorative aspects of canes and sticks – most especially the carving of those cane heads and handles.

I have tried to demonstrate a diversity of birds sufficient to allow the carver to begin with a type of wildfowl that is to his or her liking. The patterns, along with the carving and painting sequences that accompany them, are meant to instruct in the basics of cane or stick head carving. Hopefully, what is contained herein will not only provide the groundwork to allow anyone to carve a beautiful and functional cane or walking stick from the patterns provided, but will also encourage them to originate and create heirloom canes and walking sticks of their own.

Again, please be advised that the primary purpose of this book is the carving and adornment of cane handles and walking stick heads, and to that end is directed only in part at the *construction* of canes and walking sticks. Suggestions, hardware, and/or some accessories have been given or illustrated to provoke thought with respect to completion. Once a handle or head is carved, the reader is left to his own devices as to the completion of the project.

Cane/Staff History, Opinion, and Form

I would imagine that man has found it necessary to carry a cane or walking stick of some sort ever since he rose up on his spindly two legs. It takes little to encourage reaching for support when we travel with possessions on our backs as did early man. A wound or sprain would also cause an individual to look for support of some kind, and assuredly an aged person would desire the gratifying feel of something to lean on as he or she moved about.

For gatherers, a staff or stick would have been used as a tool to dig or pry with, to poke into unknown thickets, or to whack something or somebody with – as well as being used as a walking support when returning home with a gathered load.

For hunters, when not spearing game or carrying a spear at the ready in combat, what safer and more convenient way to travel with a spear than with the point up and the butt of the shaft hitting the ground with each stride? The weapon becomes a walking stick.

The cane, staff, stick, and spear were likely to be used as weapons to beat, poke, or jab with such frequency that it served that purpose as often as it was a support or a tool. He who could use any of the aforementioned with skill to hunt or fight, and prevailed in conflict or combat, gained great respect.

Gradually, the staff or spear became the symbol of strength and power – and for good reason! If I knew a guy could thump me with a big stick any time he wanted to, I doubt he would need much more than a symbol to make me stop challenging his authority and keep to my side of the cave!

And eventually, the symbol became the sign of authority and social prestige.

Ancient Egyptian rulers carried symbolic staffs.

Some ancient Grecian gods were portrayed with a staff in hand.

In the Middle Ages, pilgrims and shepherds carried long staffs or walking sticks.

A scepter (ornamental rod or staff) carried in the right hand of a king symbolized royal *power*; when carried in the king's left hand, it represented royal *justice*.

The church adopted the staff for its officials — the crosier (a long pastoral staff with a hooked handle) symbolizes the bishop's office.

The word *cane* was first applied to the walking stick after 1500, when bamboo was first used. After 1600, canes became highly fashionable for men. Made of ivory, ebony, and whalebone, as well as of wood, they had highly decorated and jeweled knob handles.

Canes were often made hollow in order to carry possessions or supplies or, in some cases, to conceal weapons. In the late seventeenth century, oak sticks were extensively used, especially by the Puritans. The cane continued in men's fashions throughout the eighteenth century. As with a woman's fan, certain rules became standard for its use. From time to time women also adopted the cane, particularly for a short time when Marie Antoinette carried the shepherd's crook.

In the nineteenth century, the cane became a mark of a professional man; the gold-headed cane was especially favored. See K. Stein, *Canes and Walking Sticks* (1973) and Jeffrey B. Snyder, *Canes: from the Seventeenth to the Twentieth Century* (1993).

Historically, canes have been articles of beauty and accent pieces for fashion and appearance. The cane, when carried socially, was a focal point of attention and added greatly to the general appearance of a person, male or female.

Unfortunately, canes have all but disappeared as a social object of fashion. With the trend towards functionality and economy, and the need for a cane primarily during a rehabilitative period, little or no thought has been given to the appearance of the cane. I think that most modern canes are incredibly ugly and undignified. It seems inappropriate to see a lady of obvious bearing and class reduced to using a crude aluminum rod with a rubber tip to support herself.

As a child, I had an aunt who had to carry a cane, and owned several, not only for different occasions, but also for different modes of dress. She would laugh and tease me because she said I paid more attention to her canes than I did to her. I was fascinated by those canes! They had the most amazing designs and inscriptions on them, yet each one possessed elegance, grace, and beauty. Years after her death, it occurred to me that those canes might still be in the family, but, I found that they had long since been sold to collectors as highly prized objects of art.

I have a friend in Florida who has a large collection of beautiful canes, yet when he had to use a cane to recover from a knee operation, the therapist told him that a "modern" cane would probably serve him better. Of course there was one that he could buy from the therapist! He bought one of the ugly aluminum modern contrivances rather than use one of those beautiful canes in his collection. He later found one from his collection that he uses to this day, and that aluminum thing is tucked away in a closet.

Heirloom Canes

A friend and fellow woodcarver asked me what I meant by an *heirloom cane*. I explained that my idea of an heirloom cane is one that remains in a family, being handed from generation to generation and continues to be used and cherished . . . so much the better if the ancestor who first used the cane was the one who carved it.

He agreed, saying that he had a plain old apple limb walking stick that his grandfather had shaped and the only adornment he had put on it was his initials. Now, his father and he had added their initials, and soon he will pass it on to his son who will keep the tradition going. He said that stick meant more to him for the memories and sentimental value than any other family item he has.

The same Grandfather that introduced me to carving and woodworking once told me that, on average, most woodcarvings serve as a decoration for only one or two generations. They will then end up in a box somewhere in an attic. Eventually such carvings will be forgotten, because they don't fit the décor of a particular individual or generation and will finally end up being sold or given away without appreciation for what the objects were or who created them.

However, if one can add functionality to a woodcarving, such an item will be admired, used, and passed from generation to generation without suffering the fate of other, strictly decorative carvings. I think hand carved and handmade canes and walking sticks fall into the latter category. They are more likely to become heirloom items that will continue to be functional, beautiful, and appreciated by generation after generation.

Parts of a Cane

The main reason I address the parts of a cane is to identify and define those parts *and* to describe the importance of each from a cane maker's point of view. As mentioned previously, a cane should not only be considered as a supporting device requiring strength and durability, but should also be considered as an object of fashion and beauty that is acceptable as an item of apparel and fashion. Realizing that each part or member of a cane has certain requirements will better allow the cane maker to design a cane or walking stick which will better satisfy all desired criteria.

Handle – the section where the cane is gripped for support. The handle will receive the most wear because it is held while being carried and when supporting the user. Of considerable importance is the finish that will be applied to the handle. If the handle is a highly detailed carving that is painted, then a protective coat of clear finish should be generously applied to protect the carved and painted handle.

Depending on preference and how the handle will enhance the cane or walking stick, the handles shown as patterns in this book will primarily be attached to form the following handle s hapes:

-*knob*: straight up on top of the cane shaft like a walking stick. The top of the cane rests in the palm while the fingers wrap around the shaft. (The Cooper's hawk pattern would be a good example of a knob handle).

-*L shape*: the cane looks like an upside down "L" and the short foot of the L is held for support. (The Sandhill Crane Pattern is an example of a pattern that is used as an L-shaped handle).

-*T shape*: the handle extends across the cane shaft, making it look like a modified "T" and the cross of the T is held for support. (The Merganser pattern could be used as a T-shaped handle).

-*C shape*: the handle loops off the top of the cane shaft forming a "C" shape. This is the standard shape we think of when we think of a cane. (The Ring-neck Pheasant pattern is a modified C shape, and if the loop of the C were widened, it would be more of conventional C shaped handle).

On sectionally constructed canes, including the majority of canes in this book, the handle will be carved separately and added to the shaft upon completion. Consideration must be given to how handle and shaft will be joined before assembly. Thought must be given to which joint will offer the most strength and best appearance. Will the cane have a removable head or a permanently fixed one? Considerations such as how the joint will be accomplished may make a big difference in the appearance of the cane when it is complete. If the joint is to be doweled and glued, give careful thought to assembly and the steps required to achieve the final joining. Usually, fitting the handle rough-out to the shaft of the cane *before* carving alleviates any problem not considered later after the head carving is complete.

Joint – usually the area where the handle and the cane shaft join. The joint between the handle and the cane shaft must be of sufficient strength to safely support the user. The cane maker must give careful consideration to how the handle and staff are joined – the two strongest methods are a doweled and glued butt joint using a hardwood or metal dowel, or a socketed joint, usually where the staff enters a flat bottomed hole in the handle.

The joint should be considered the weakest point of the cane, due to the directional change of the grain and/or the joining process. A poorly designed cane will usually break at the joint due to improper or inadequate joinery. The type of joining process depends on where the joint falls between the handle and the shaft.

A socket joint is usually used where the handle can afford a hole of corresponding size to accept the shaft. If possible, a dowel is added to extend strength into the handle.

A butt joint is usually found on a cane where the handle is in line with the shaft. Such a joint normally requires being pinned with a metal or hardwood dowel in addition to being glued.

A screw joint utilizes commercially prepared cane hardware. This particular method of joining the head to the shaft is one of my favorites, because I can change the carved head on a cane or walking stick as the mood suits me.

Collar – a collar can be made of metal, wood, horn, or plastic, and is placed over or on the seam of a joint. There are generally three reasons for the appearance of a collar on a cane, and the motivations behind using a particular collar may involve all three. First, for looks, to give attraction to the cane by using materials with colors that enhance or oppose the colors used in the handle and shaft. Second, to hide any disparity in the construction of the joint between the handle and the shaft. Third, the collar is used to inscribe the name of the owner of the cane. Heirloom canes were provided with collars (usually silver) wide enough to accept several generations of owners' names.

Shaft or Staff – the supporting length of a cane, the shaft can be ornamented or plain. A plain shaft will often draw attention to the shape or carving of the handle; whereas, the shape of some handles will dictate the continuance of the handle design, either partially down the shaft or, on some, along the full length of the shaft. This balance of design, of color, and of form allows the cane craftsman to best demonstrate his or her skill and knowledge of the craft.

Traditionally, we think of a cane as measuring 36-inches long and under, and a walking stick as 48-inches and over, depending on the user's height.

Tip – the tip of the cane usually refers to an added part at the bottom of the cane. Seldom is a well-made cane left without a protective covering over the wooden end of the shaft. Most modern canes will possess a rubber tip with a circular tread of some kind to prevent the cane tip from sliding on smooth surfaces such as floors, pavement, or ledges. Some may have a collared metal tip with a replaceable rubber insert that is screwed in or held within the tip by friction. Many formal canes will have a completely metal tip which offers much less traction on the surfaces mentioned above, but will last for generations. There are screw-in cane tips and points that can be interchanged for use in winter or cold weather when the metal point adapts itself very well to use on ice or snow (see *cane hardware*). However, I suggest that the point tip be replaced with the rubber tip adapter before the cane is used indoors . . . or even brought indoors. One day I ran back through the house to get a piece of hiking gear I had forgotten, and I found that a metal point on a walking stick really doesn't help the walk across an inlaid linoleum floor – nor does it help a marriage!

Sizing Canes & Walking Sticks

How to Measure a Cane

While wearing your normal footwear, stand against the wall with arms hanging comfortably at your sides. Measure the distance from the floor to the crease of the wrist. This is the perfect height for your cane. While grasping a cane and standing in a normal upright position, the forearm should form an approximate 30° angle with the ground.

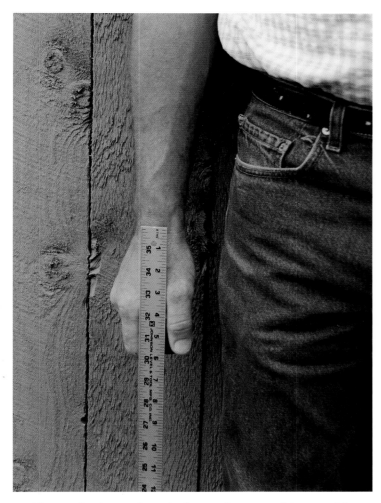

Measure the distance from the floor to the crease of the wrist. This is the perfect height for your cane.

For some reason, I found it stated that for people over 70 it is acceptable to have the cane length 2 or 3 inches longer than the above measurement. No precise reason was given for why a cane 2 to 3 inches longer was recommended for persons of that particular age and over. My mother-in-law is 94 years old and still as active as someone 60 or 65, and when I measured her for a cane, she much preferred a cane two inches longer than the supposed optimum length. She goes up and down stairs (she lives alone in a three story colonial house), walks across streets, and strolls along sidewalks with a cane that I would have thought ill-fitting.

This may have to do with the fact that a younger person stands more erect, and an older person leans forward, changing the balance point. Some older folks use the cane more for

While grasping a cane and standing in a normal upright position, the forearm should form an approximate 30° angle with the ground.

balance than for support, so the longer cane may offer a greater sense and ease of balance. I have observed large men who have an injury or a crippled leg whose main concern was for support rather than balance. To a man, they preferred properly fit canes that came to the wrist-line or slightly below so they could throw weight onto the cane with a stiff arm.

How to Measure a Walking Stick

To determine the proper location for the placement of the hand, a handgrip, or wrapping on a walking stick, take a long stick, a length of closet rod, or a broom or rake held upside down and grasp it at a comfortable height. To be sure it is right, walk around with your hand held at that position, using this rod as you would use a walking stick while walking or hiking. If it feels comfortable with your hand at that height, measure from the top of your hand to the floor, and use that measurement to affix the wrapping or carved handgrip to your walking stick. Since this measurement will be the height of the stick to the top of the *handgrip*, when mounting the walking stick patterns from this book, there will be approximately 5" to 7" of additional carved stick above the top of the handgrip.

Remember, the top of the handgrip has nothing to do with the portion of the *walking stick* that is carved from a pattern in this book, or any other you may want to carve, so the hand and handgrip will be below the carved portion.

To determine the proper location for the placement of a handgrip or wrapping on a walking stick, take a long stick, a length of closet rod, or a broom or rake held upside down and grasp it at a comfortable height.

Depending on the type of handgrip that you plan to apply to your stick, you will want to honor *at least* the measurement you took off the broom or rake handle. If carving a handgrip for a walking stick, I often make it longer in case I want to shift my grip (usually downward) on a leisurely walk. I also make the handgrip for a walking stick a bit longer so it will fit others besides myself. I keep several at my woodcarving school so students can use them to walk about the trails in their free time.

However, if I am carving a hiking or trekking stick, I will adhere more closely to the measurement from the broom handle, as I will have a wrist strap. The strap will be adjusted to the handgrip area to keep my hand more or less anchored while I walk with a more measured gait.

A general measurement check for any walking stick is one where the stick will "top off" even with the shoulder joint.

Thanks to my son, Jeffrey Russell for modeling the cane/stick measuring sequences.

Wood Selection

For any green wood blanks that I use for canes, I use trees or saplings directly from my mountain. This wood can come from any of the deciduous (leaf bearing trees) that I find up there — such as Red or White Oak, Hard Maple, Red Maple, Basswood, Ash, Poplar, Tamarack, Butternut, Beech, Yellow and White Birch — to conifers (cone bearing trees), such as Hemlock, Pine, Spruce, or Balsam.

I select wood for my canes from whichever tree, sapling, or milled wood will best satisfy the color, shape, durability, and/or workability for any cane that I am carving.

Short of Balsa, I don't think there is a wood that exists that is not suitable for a cane shaft, a cane handle, or a walking stick. If the handle is carved of a softer wood, such as Tupelo, care should be taken to ensure that detail and texturing is cut deep enough, and a hard protective finish is used to prevent detail wearing away.

The types of wood used for projects shown in the carving sequences for this book were milled Tupelo for the Bald Eagle, milled Walnut for the Mallard Duck, and a Red Maple tree for the Flamingo limb/trunk blank.

Selecting Natural Cane and Walking Stick Blanks

I find many bird shapes and waterfowl heads in natural sapling and tree bends. Many of the patterns found in this book have been carved from saplings that were found on one of the many amblings through my woods. There is nothing that compares to time enjoyed with my two golden retrievers as we wander about our mountain on a beautiful and brisk fall day in search of carving stock for canes and walking sticks. They do more searching for woodcock than they do for wood stock, but they at least give passing interest to much of what I stop to examine.

Wandering over our mountain on a beautiful and brisk fall day, searching for carving stock for canes and walking sticks.

The golden retrievers do more searching for woodcock than they do for wood stock, but they at least give passing interest to much of what I stop to examine.

Whenever I go walking in the woods, I look for saplings that are growing out of the sides of banks or steep slopes. As the young tree struggles to grow toward the sky, it must first establish a root system with a taproot (main root). They grow out of the side of the bank almost in a horizontal position before heading skyward. The steeper the bank or slope, the more acute the angle that the sapling must form in order to begin growing in a vertical position.

The steeper the bank or slope, the more acute the angle between the root and the trunk that the sapling must form in order to grow in a vertical position.

Another place to look for saplings with a root structure that is bent is along the tops of ledges and cliffs where shallow earth covering over the ledge has allowed a sapling to take root. The root will follow along the line of the shallow earth and the ledge as the tree grows straight up, forming an excellent shape for a cane.

The angle that is formed by the sapling's effort to grow upward very often will form an excellent bend from which to shape the handle of a cane, the head of a walking stick, or even the hook for a staff.

This bend provides an excellent shape into which the cane or stick carver can create or design any number of interesting and creative shapes to carve. A very common one of course, is a snake shape. I couldn't hazard a guess as to how many snake shapes have been fashioned from these natural formations. Although the snake is not one of my favorite animals, the curves and scale patterns that can be worked into a carving such as this do make a beautiful cane or walking stick.

Some of the nut trees offer limbs that are straight and long enough to create beautiful canes (with bends included) and walking sticks. I always look for walnut and butternut trees that are in need of pruning, and very often I have gathered several suitable cane and stick blanks plus stock for many handles from just one tree – and the owner was very happy to get his tree pruned.

Small groves of poplar saplings are scattered over my land and the neighboring farmland. These little groves of straight "sticks" provide a great selection of walking sticks to carve, and thinning also improves the health of the grove.

A poplar grove.

When the overall grove grows too large to harvest walking sticks, I move to the edges of the grove and find new saplings.

Sumac groves also provide another source for beautiful stick shafts. When the bark is removed from the sumac, it reveals layers of cream, green, and brown wood that makes for some interesting carvings as the shape of the carving is relieved away.

Limb and Trunk Blanks

Whenever I see a tree that has been blown down, is being cut down, or one that has been selected for firewood, such as the one featured, I do my best to be on hand while it is being cut, and either buy some limb and trunk sections or offer to cut it down and cut it up for the owner. I am usually rewarded with six or eight limb/trunk cane blanks (and a lot of needed exercise!).

The trick to acquiring a good limb/trunk cane blank is to find a tree with branches that grow as near parallel with the trunk as possible. When cut, the limb is left attached to a portion of the trunk which provides the stock to shape a handle or decorative head, while the limb serves as the shaft.

Creating a Limb/Trunk Cane Blank

2. Cut the limb longer than required for a cane shaft, and cut enough of the trunk above and below the joint of the limb to satisfy the shape and size requirements of the handle you wish to carve.

1. Select a tree with a limb that grows as close to parallel with the trunk as possible and is of a size that will work well as a cane shaft. Choose a branch that will suit the size of the cane handle you wish to carve, keeping in mind what you intend to do with it. For example, if you wish to remove the bark and uniformly round the shaft, you will want to choose a branch slightly larger than one where you intend to keep the branch in a natural state.

I know of no "rule of thumb" to sizing a shaft to a handle. I think it pretty much lies in the eye of the person creating the cane. I have seen graceful handles on virtual "clubs" and I have seen monster handles on "toothpicks." I try to make my combinations look fluid and balanced.

3. **Right:** With a chainsaw, carefully cut a slab from the trunk that will accommodate the width of the handle you wish to carve. Choose a direction off the limb joint for the slab that will best suit the way the limb joins the trunk, will best fit your pattern, and will provide the strongest, most attractive grain pattern for the handle.

4. A slabbed trunk and limb section ready to receive a pattern outline.

5. Orient the pattern on the trunk slab in a manner that will best bring the pattern lines to the limb. The pattern used for this blank was the flamingo pattern featured in this book.

6. Cut the pattern outline (side view) with a band saw. There are times when cutting the top view is also possible on the band saw, but usually the blank shaft gets in the way and prevents accurate cutting. I have come to prefer removing stock for the top view to desired thickness, then shaping by hand.

7. Since the blank was taken from a newly cut tree (red maple) and was "green" enough to contain a goodly amount of sap, to prevent checking or splitting, the handle portion was soaked in Pentacryl® for twenty-four hours to stabilize the grain structure. Pentacryl will completely penetrate a carving blank this size within that twenty-four-hour period (see Pentacryl definition and specifications below).

11

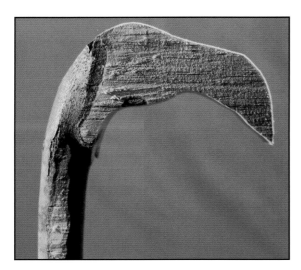

8. The stabilized limb & trunk cane blank is ready to carve. After the cane blank handle has soaked in wood stabilizer for 24 hours, I wipe it dry, then wash the entire area with lacquer thinner, and allow the blank to dry for another 24 hours.

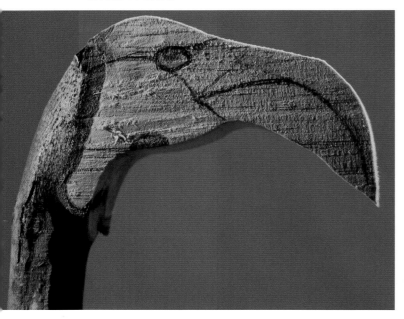

9. Penciled contours.

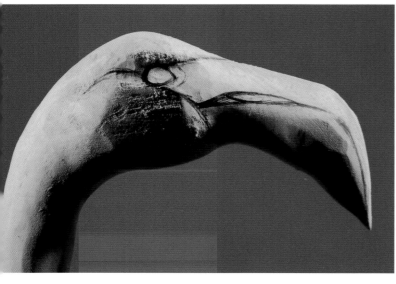

10. Rough shaped head. Redraw eyes, nostrils, and beak.

11. Rough carved and smoothed limb/trunk blank ready for finish detailing, texturing, and setting eyes. Add details, texturing, and eyes as per instructions found in *Finish Carving and Detailing* under Carving the Bald Eagle on page 27.

Pentacryl Defined

Pentacryl was originally developed for the treatment of waterlogged wood, but has since become an invaluable resource for woodcarvers, woodturners, and woodworkers as it keeps green wood from cracking and splitting. Pentacryl is a compound of siliconized polymers that does not discolor wood, is non-hydroscopic (does not gather moisture), and will not oxidize, decompose, or migrate in wood when exposed to different degrees of temperature and/or relative humidity.

Pentacryl can be applied by brushing, spraying, or soaking. I find soaking to be the most beneficial, not only with regard to penetration, but to time, in that I can put several green and freshly cut cane blanks in a container of the fluid at once, and go on to other things while waiting for it to penetrate. Incidentally, wood does not have to be completely saturated with the liquid to be stabilized.

Wood treated with Pentacryl will accept most finishes, whether acrylic or oil based. The key to success with the application of *any* finish, however, is that the Pentacryl surface must be as dry as possible prior to application. As an alternative, stain added to Pentacryl will color a carving blank while it stabilizes the wood structure. The depth of color obtained depends on the amount of stain added.

Technical data, specifications, and retailer listings can be obtained from:

Preservation Solutions
1060 Bunker Hill Road
Jefferson, Maine 04348

Speaking of cutting natural walking sticks, if you don't own the property where you have located saplings, it would be a good idea to get permission from the landowner to cut one or two before you "cut and run," so to speak! I was headed across a property that I had permission to deer hunt on — although this time armed with a shovel and axe — when the caretaker drove out and asked where I was going with the tools. I explained what I intended to do, and he explained what I was NOT going to do until we checked with the owner, and the venture ended for that day.

Shaping Shafts

Natural Shafts

The easiest shaft to create comes from a length of sapling of preferred diameter cut to the desired length. Choose one as straight as possible; the more bends there are in the shaft, the more vibration that is delivered to the wrist, whether in a cane or a walking stick. With the bark left on, the sapling shaft lends itself very well to bird, animal, and nature carving themes. The first Cardinal walking stick that I carved from the pattern shown in this book was carved from a natural sapling, and I left bark on the entire length of the shaft, leaving only natural wood for the carved cardinal stick head, and the handle/thong area.

To ensure that the bark will adhere to the shaft over time, I seal the entire shaft with thinned flat lacquer to seal and lock it into place. I use several coats of automotive lacquer thinned 50% with lacquer thinner.

Most of the shafts I use have had the bark removed from them — especially if I plan to carve along the length of the shaft. I use a spoke shave or a draw knife to strip the bark away, then I allow the shaft to dry for a while if the shaft has been cut in the spring or summer while sap is flowing in the sapling. A drier shaft is easier to work with than a freshly cut wet shaft. I have found the best time to cut saplings for walking sticks is during the late fall or winter when the sap has stopped flowing.

Sawn Shaft

An attractive shaft can be made by first rip sawing (cutting along the length with the grain) a length of stock to an octagonal shape. This is accomplished by first sawing the stock square, then setting the saw blade at a 45° angle, and ripping all four corners to form the eight equal sides of an octagon. The eight flats of the shaft can then be smoothed by running opposing sides through a planer with the planer head set to the desired thickness, or the entire shaft can be hand sanded using a sanding block while exercising care to keep the surfaces flat and uniform.

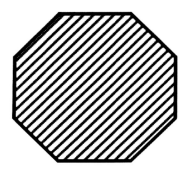

Octagonal cross-section of a cane shaft. An octagonal cane shaft is shaped by first sawing the stock square, then setting the saw blade at a 45° angle and ripping all four corners to form the eight equal sides of an octagon.

This type of staff will require the later addition of the cane or stick head (and/or handle). However, for a walking stick, it allows the shaft to be shaped to full length without joinery anywhere along its length. I think shaping a shaft using this method gives the cane a more formal look. I especially like to "dress" a cane shaft with an opposing colored tip and collar before I add a handle — for example, a walnut shaft with maple collar and tip.

Turned Shaft

Many shafts for canes and walking sticks are turned on a lathe. This method affords the stick or cane maker the greatest variety and choice of shaft. The shaft of a cane can be turned tapered or straight, it can be ornamented with grooves or raised rings, and, finally, it can be finish coated . . . all done while in place on the lathe.

I have not yet been able to find (nor afford) a non-commercial lathe with a bed long enough to turn the full length of a walking stick shaft (60"-65").

I have tried to purchase 60 inch tapered shafts for walking sticks from companies that turn the larger decorative posts for porches and railings. However, understandably, the price was prohibitive for the few pieces that I wanted.

To date, I have used two methods to create walking stick shafts on a short-bed lathe (36" length). One method is to turn half-lengths of the shaft and join them with a doweled glue joint (usually with a fancy wood spacer between them). The second method is to make a "take-down" screw joint which allows the user to assemble and disassemble the walking stick in the same manner that one would assemble a pool cue.

While many of the hikers and outdoors-folks prefer the takedown type shaft because it can be disassembled and easily transported, most people who just take a daily walk around the neighborhood prefer the fixed length of a walking stick because it is usually left leaning in the same place each day (in a corner, a coat closet, behind a door) where it provides easy access.

Most of the cane heads and walking stick heads that I carve are screw-on heads with a female threaded insert. I like the idea of being able to use the same shaft with different heads that I have carved. When I go for a walk or a hike, I enjoy having a different subject with me each time. Most importantly, when I walk or hike, I usually have my camera with me, and the threaded metal pin that sticks out of the top of the walking stick shaft and screws into the stick head, also fits my camera. All I have to do is unscrew the carved head, screw on my camera, and I have a nice monopod with which to steady my camera.

When turning a walking stick that I intend to use as a camera monopod, I turn a handle area that will have finger grooves. These grooves not only allow a tangible grip while the camera is mounted, but provide a comfortable handle to grasp while hiking. A common mistake for beginning stick makers is to leave the shaft too thick and too heavy to be a comfort while in use. The finished stick must be an object of function as well as one of beauty.

Routed Shaft

A routed shaft is a shaft that begins as a long square stick for a blank and all four corners are routed (shaped) with a router and the bit shape of choice. Before attempting to route a shaft for a cane or walking stick, I provide additional support for the router. This support is usually nothing more than another piece of stock of equal thickness to the shaft blank that is clamped or screwed to the bench alongside the shaft blank. Once the blank is clamped in place, the blank and the adjacent piece of stock both act as supporting surfaces for the router to ride on. The "fixture" supports the shaft blank while I shape each corner with whatever router bit shape I have selected.

Some bit shapes that lend themselves very well to shaping this type of shaft are quarter round, quarter concave, 45-degree bevel, or even some of the more ornate router bit shapes that will satisfy the corner shaping that you might prefer on the shaft. Always use bits with roller bearings on them, or use an edge guide on your router.

A floor-mounted shaper can also be used to shape the edges of this type of cane shaft, but I find the router more versatile if I am making a tapered cane shaft. The shaper will give as fine a finish, but the main problem is setting the hold down guides properly and feeding the shaft by the cutter head. Even with push sticks I don't like my hands/fingers that close to that cutter head!

Tool Handle Shaft

I must admit that I have made some rather remarkable walking sticks and canes with carved heads from unfinished broom, mop, and rake handles that I have found at the local hardware store. I have also made several nice walking sticks and canes from old pool cues. Pool cue walking sticks can be easily unscrewed and stored in an auto for transportation. Even better for carrying the pool cue cane is the partitioned box that the cue came in.

It is a simple chore to drill a hole the same size as the broomstick in the bottom of the carved stick head and glue the head to the stick. After finish is applied to the stick, I wrap the grip area with a rawhide thong or a wide leather flat lace to provide a handgrip (with or without a wrist loop). After adding a rubber crutch or cane tip, the project is complete.

Don't be afraid to "collar" the tip down as necessary to make the rubber crutch or cane tip fit. The fit should be as snug as possible, but not left so big as to eventually split the rubber tip from hard use and/or the user leaning on it.

Tools

Joinery Tools & Accessories

Tenon Cutters

Tenon cutters: These cutters are designed to run vibration free while being driven by an electric drill. They cut a nice smooth tenon with a slight radius on the shoulder. These cutters offer a broad range of sizes to satisfy about any size shaft that would be used for a cane or walking stick. There are mini sizes (1/4", 3/8", ½", 9/16") and larger sizes (5/8", 3/4", 7/8", 1", 1 ½", 2") – with 5/8" through 1" most suitable for cane and stick making. They are not for use in a drill press – the smaller sizes (up to 1-inch) are used in an electric drill with a 3/8-inch or larger chuck, and the larger sizes are for use in an electric hand drill with a ½-inch chuck.

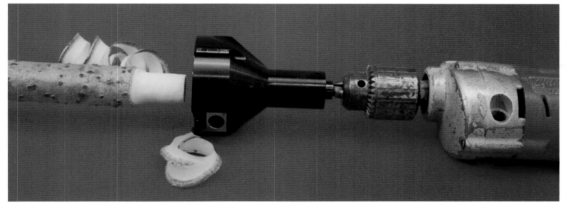

A tenon cut with a hand drill. I have used these cutters for everything from furniture making and repair to cane and walking stick construction. These bits will easily shape a male end on a piece of wood stock that will fit a corresponding hole to make an extremely strong and tidy joint for either canes, walking sticks, or furniture.

Once the male end is made, a hole of corresponding size is drilled using a Forstner drill bit (see the following photo), and the two are glue joined to make a very secure and attractive joint. I have used them time and time again to join cane and stick heads.

Forstner Bits

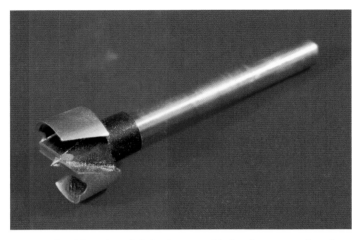

Forstner Bit: These bits drill flat-bottomed holes that accept dowels or tenoned ends of shafts to form a strong joint when glued. Forstner bits are available in a wide range of sizes.

Economically, sets of Forstner bits are far cheaper to buy than individual bits.

The Tenon Cutters and Forstner Bits featured above are available from:

Lee Valley Tools Ltd.
12 East River Street
Ogdensburg, New York 13669.

All preparation for joinery (joining a handle or head to a shaft) should be fitted and complete before cutting or carving the head/handle and shaft components of a cane or walking stick. It is much easier to drill and fit rough squared stock than it is to try to work around a beautifully carved handle and shaped shaft. This applies to any case whether it be a piece of square stock to be turned on the lathe, squared stock to be corner-shaped with a router or shaper, or even a natural sapling to be used for a walking stick. *Always* fit the roughed out components to be joined before carving and finish shaping.

Hardware and Accessories

Couplers

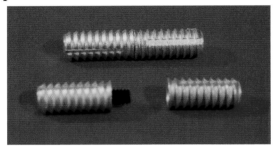

Couplers are excellent for joining the handle of a cane to a cane shaft, or the carved head of a walking stick to a shaft. With a coupler, additional length can be added to a cane shaft to convert it to a walking stick in the same manner that a pool cue is screwed together. A walking stick with a coupler can be easily broken down for easy transport or stowage in a carrying case.

The coupler shown is an assembly consisting of two 1-inch long by 7/16-inch diameter nuts connected by a $\frac{1}{4}$-20 threaded joining screw.

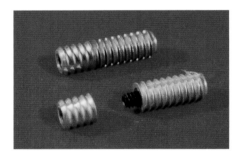

A walking stick can easily be converted to a camera mount monopod by unscrewing the carved stick head and mounting a camera on the exposed threaded screw sticking up from the center of the shaft of the walking stick. These camera mount couplers have two 7/16-inch diameter nuts (one $\frac{1}{2}$-inch long and the other 1-inch long), and are joined by a $\frac{1}{4}$-20 threaded stud. *Note: Both video cameras and 35mm cameras have $\frac{1}{4}$-20 threaded mounting holes.*

I find a camera mount invaluable when I am doing photography for carving references at zoos, sanctuaries, game refuges, or in any situation where I need a good stable support for shooting a photograph.

Joining Plates

Joining plates are available with 1-inch and $\frac{3}{4}$-inch plates. These are excellent for those who wish to make segmented canes or walking sticks, or desire hardware for mounting handles to canes or heads to walking sticks. When joined, the brass plate makes a very attractive spacer between the two pieces being joined.

Cane Tips

Cane tips are added to the tips (bottoms) of cane shafts to prevent wear and eroding of the cane shaft as it is placed repeatedly against the ground. In addition to protection, the tip also should provide a degree of traction to prevent the cane from sliding out from under the weight applied by the user.

The most common tips are the rubber crutch-type tips that slide easily on the cane shaft and are held in place by friction and/or a drop of super glue. These rubber tips are available in a variety of sizes and colors (predominately black, brown, or white). The ones shown here were purchased at a flea market for from thirty-cents to sixty-cents apiece. The larger ones are well suited for use on the ends of larger walking sticks.

The most common tips are the rubber crutch-type tips that easily slide on the cane shaft and are held in place by friction and/or a drop of super glue.

To add more of an air of quality to a cane, brass or other metal tips are an excellent choice. The usual choice is brass, but I have had stainless steel tips turned for canes where I wanted a silver color to enhance the look of the wood. On several occasions, I even made silver tips from jewelry stock for cane tips where the cane was never to be used, but was simply added to a collection. As previously stated, the more commonly used metal for a tip is brass.

A so-called traditional British cane tip is available which is made from drawn brass with a steel disc welded to the bottom to prevent wear. These tips are approximately 1-inch high, are slightly tapered, and are usually available in 9/16-inch, 5/8-inch, and ¾-inch sizes. The tip is set with epoxy, a brass pin, or a brad. These tips add greatly to the beauty and presentation of a cane, but for those who would depend on a cane for function and support, I have concerns about the lack of traction due to the smoothness of the steel-plated tip.

A so-called traditional British cane tip is available which is made from drawn brass with a steel disc welded to the bottom to prevent wear.

The best brass cane tips are machine-turned from bar stock to ensure quality and uniformity, and are then fitted with replaceable rubber tips that provide the desired traction. This is my choice for the majority of the canes that I create that have metal tips. They are ¾-inch in length and fit cane shaft ends with a diameter of 5/8-inch or larger. The tip has a heavy-duty replaceable rubber tip and a fixing screw.

The best brass cane tips are machine-turned from bar stock to ensure quality and uniformity, and are then fitted with replaceable rubber tips that provide the desired traction.

An excellent and versatile tip for a staff or walking stick is a brass tip that has not only a rubber tip for path or sidewalk walking, but has an interchangeable stainless steel tip that can be added for stream walking or mountain trekking. These tips are 1 ¼-inches long, and fit a shaft end with a diameter of ¾-inch or larger. They are scored internally to provide a mechanical lock for gluing and have internally chamfered lips for a snug fit. For extreme use, the addition of a pin should be considered — if you subject the tip of a walking stick to the horrors of water, mud, gravel, ice, and snow that I do.

An excellent and versatile tip for a staff or walking stick is a brass tip that has not only a rubber tip for path or sidewalk walking, but has an interchangeable stainless steel tip that can be added for stream walking or mountain trekking.

The author wishes to thank Lee Valley Tools Ltd., 12 East River Street, Ogdensburg, New York 13669, for providing all the cane hardware featured above.

Carving Tools & Machines

Flexible Shaft Machine

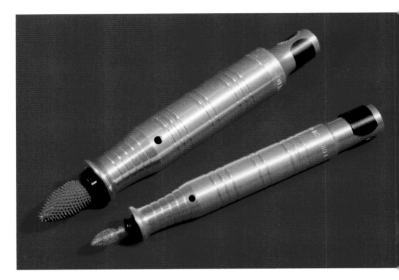

A large and small hand piece make reducing and shaping stock much easier.

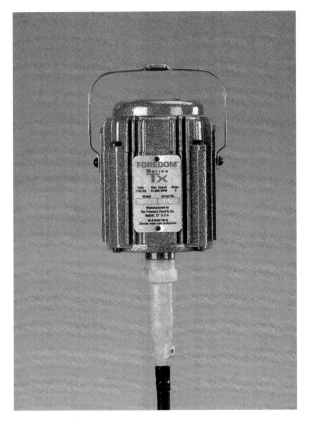

Foredom TX Machine with forward and reverse.

Micromotor Machine

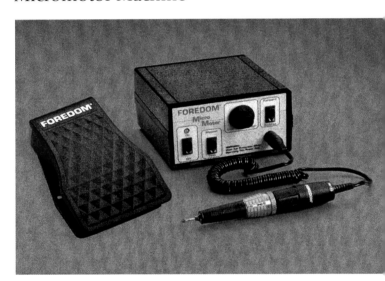

Foredom #1045 45,000 RPM Micromotor Machine.

The Flexible shaft machine used to rough out and shape the projects in this book is the Foredom TX Machine with forward and reverse. Reverse is not that important for the right-handed carver, but is of utmost importance to the left-handed carver. To allow the left-handed carver the same rotational privilege as the right-hander, the machine should be run in reverse. By necessity, the bit should be turning toward the carver, whether left or right handed. In order for the left-hander to get the machine to run toward him, the machine must be running in reverse. This allows monitoring of the bottom of the bit where the cut is taking place, and the left-hander is not fighting the direction of the bit that would try to run away from him if it were not in reverse.

This machine provides the power necessary to rough out any band-sawn carving blank with ease and accuracy when provided with the proper bit. A large and small hand piece make reducing and shaping stock much easier – the large hand piece easily takes care of wasting away and rough shaping, and the smaller hand piece is a more convenient size for continued wasting away and the refining of rough shaped details.

This particular machine is the Foredom 1045 micromotor that revolves at 45,000 rpm (revolutions per minute). The motor in this machine is definitely not for roughing out large shapes as is the flexible shaft featured above, but the high speed of this machine and the range of freedom of the hand piece allow for fine detailing and, generally, a smoother cut. This is the machine of choice for all the light carving, detailing, and texturing used on the projects throughout this book.

For a catalog of Foredom machines, bits, and accessories, contact:

Foredom Electric Company
16 Stony Hill Road
Bethel, Connecticut 06801-1039

Wood Burning

Burning Pens

The burning bits used throughout this book are a medium wide skew, a small sharp skew, and a large and small bent unsharpened skew to outline feathers.

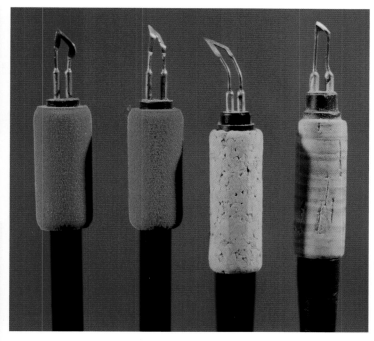

A medium wide skew; a small sharp skew; and a large and small bent unsharpened skew to outline feathers.

Wood burning pens with blue heat guards are manufactured by:

SMC Enterprises
236 Mimi Street
Cadiz, Kentucky 42211

while pens with cork heat guards are made by:

Colwood Electronics, Inc
15 Meridian Road
Eatontown, New Jersey 07724

Control Box

A control box must generate an even and constant source of power to the pen and have a quick recovery time as the pen is repeatedly cooled during the texturing process. At a minimum, features I look for on the face of the box are an ON/OFF switch separate from a heat adjustment indicator and a pilot light that tells me whether the unit is on or off.

Some boxes have the ON/OFF switch and heat setting indication combined on one knob. For me, the heat setting indicator should be separate from the ON/OFF switch simply because once I begin burn texturing, I usually have occasion to turn the unit off and on several times during the course of texturing the project. I want the setting to be the same each time I turn the unit back on,

and unless I can leave it set in the same place, most of the time I can't remember what setting it was on when I turned it off.

I like a pilot light on the control face of the unit because there are times when I forget to turn the unit off, and a brightly lit pilot light warns me that the unit is *not* off. The last thing I do anytime that I finish work in the studio is to scan my work area for a lit pilot light.

I also like the control box shown for the fact that it is small, light, and very portable, yet has enough power to satisfy the demands of my heaviest pens. It performs well enough that every carving station at my woodcarving school is equipped with one. The control box is also manufactured by *SMC Enterprises*.

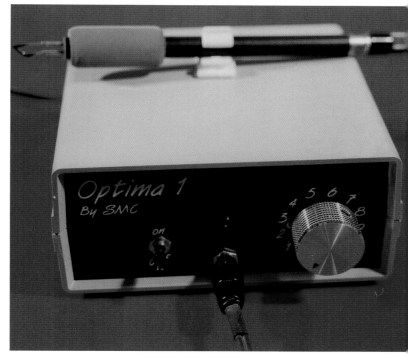

Wood burning control box.

Bits & Bit Use

Bit Use

Selection of the wrong bit for a particular function is usually the reason many beginning woodcarvers give up on a project, or even give up on power carving. If the bit doesn't function as it should, and give the desired result, then the carver is wasting time, as well as effort and materials. Having stated all of this, let me hasten to say that in some cases, what will function perfectly for one carver won't do as well for another, due to carving technique and/or machinery. It remains for the individual to experiment and practice to learn how bits function and how bits are used to achieve desired results.

Bits Used for Projects

Roughing

Carbide Cutters (Coarse (teal color) and Fine (gold color)).

Type	Shape	Grit	Function
Carbide Burr 1/4" shaft	Cylinder	Coarse Or Fine	Wasting on flats with side. V-cuts with top corner.
Carbide Burr 1/4" shaft	Flame	Coarse Or Fine	V-cuts, U-cuts, flat and round contouring.

Shaping

Carbide Cutters (Coarse (teal color) and Fine (gold color)).

Type	Shape	Grit	Function
Carbide Burr 1/8" shaft	Flame	Coarse Or Fine	Initiating smaller cuts/ shapes and/or refining rough shapes, V-cuts, U-cuts, and contours.
Carbide Burr 3/32" shaft	Flame	Coarse Or Fine	Initiating smaller cuts/ shapes and further defining existing cuts, shapes, and contours.

Detailing

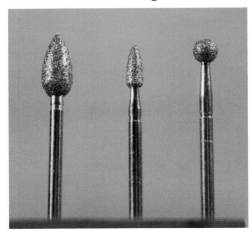

Ruby Carvers.

Type	Shape	Grit	Function
Ruby Carver 3/32" shaft	Flame 1/4" x 3/8"	Medium	General wasting away and refining shape.
Ruby Carver 3/32" shaft	Flame 1/8" x 3/8"	Fine	Defining and detailing shape.
Ruby Carver 3/32" shaft	Ball 1/8" dia.	Fine	Outlining and reducing shape, pre-texturing, cutting eyeholes.

Diamond Bits.

Type	Shape	Grit	Function
Diamond Bit 3/32" shaft	Flame 1/16" x 1/4"	Fine	Undercutting feathers, fine shaping, and detailing.
Diamond Bit 3/32" shaft	Ball 1/16" dia.	Fine	Cutting nostrils, round shaping.
Diamond Bit 3/32" shaft	Inverted Cone 1/16" dia.	Fine	Fine Texturing.
Diamond Bit 3/32" shaft	Inverted Cone 1/8" dia.	Fine	Coarse Texturing.

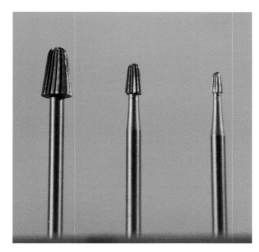

Steel Bits.

Type	Shape	Grit	Function
Steel Bit 3/32" shaft	Tapered 3/16" x 3/8"	Medium	Outlining & shaping large feathers.
Steel Bit 3/32" shaft	Tapered 1/8" x 5/16"	Medium	Outlining & shaping medium feathers.
Steel Bit 3/32" shaft	Tapered 1/16" x 1/4"	Medium	Outlining & shaping small feathers.

Texturing

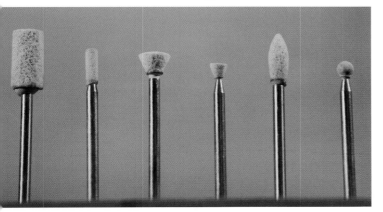

Stone Bits.

Type	Shape	Grit	Function
Stone Bit 3/32" shaft	Large Cylinder 3/16" x 5/8"	Fine	Texturing larger scale feathers.
Stone Bit 3/32" shaft	Small Cylinder 3/32" x 5/16"	Fine	Texturing smaller scale feathers.
Stone Bit 3/32" shaft	Inverted Cone 3/16" dia.	Fine	Texturing larger scale feathers.
Stone Bit 3/32" shaft	Inverted Cone . 1/8" dia	Fine	Texturing smaller scale feathers.
Stone Bit 3/32" shaft	Flame 1/8" x 3/8"	Fine	Outlining, shaping, and smoothing feathers.
Stone Bit 3/32" shaft	Ball 1/8" dia.	Fine	Pre-texturing feathers.

Smoothing

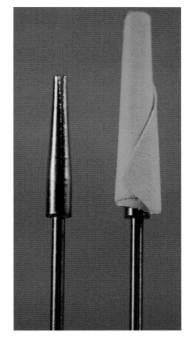

Tapered Sanding Mandrel (mandrel, loaded mandrel).

Type	Shape	Grit	Function
Sanding Mandrel 3/32" shaft	Tapered		Smaller smoothing operations, individual feathers, feather groups. General surface and shape smoothing.

Cylinder Sanding Mandrel (small 1/2" x 2").

Type	Shape	Grit	Function
Sanding Mandrel 1/4" Shaft	Cylinder 1/2" x 2"		Smoothing intermediate shapes, contours, and surfaces.

Cleaning

Rotary Brush.

Type	Shape	Grit	Function
Rotary Brush 3/32" shaft	Poly Bristle 1" dia. or larger		Cleaning textured surfaces prior to applying sealer and finishes.

The roughing bits featured throughout this book were provided by:

L. R. Oliver & Co, Inc.
9974 Dixie Highway
Fair Haven, Michigan 48023-2818

All other bits were provided by:
The Foredom Electric Co.
16 Stony Hill Road
Bethel, Connecticut 06801-1029

Safety

Improper handling of the carving machines illustrated in this book can certainly result in nasty cuts or grind marks on your hands, arms, or legs (should you drop the hand piece in your lap). But, for the most part, I would not consider these life threatening. What is extremely life threatening, with prolonged practice, is the inhalation of the fine dust created by the carving process, whether during roughing, shaping, sanding, or texturing.

As carvers, we usually take time to keep our work areas clean of the wood dust, shavings, and other debris generated by the wasting away process connected with the carving project. Unfortunately, we often fail to deal with what is most dangerous to our health – the air-laden particles of wood dust that we can't see, and readily inhale without proper protection.

To this end, make every effort to secure a work position that affords *more* than adequate dust collection.

-Always wear a dust mask.

-Provide proper ventilation, even if it is nothing more than a fan blowing across and away from the front of your work area and out a door or window or toward a vacuum.

-Use a dust collection system that is sufficient to exchange the air in your work area so as to prevent a concentration of air-borne particles.

Cylinder Sanding Mandrel (large ¾" x 3").

Type	Shape	Grit	Function
Sanding Mandrel ¼" shaft	Cylinder ¾" x 3"		Smoothing larger shapes, contours, and surfaces.

22

Carving Details

Project One
Carving the Bald Eagle

Preparing the Carving Block

Whenever possible, transfer the pattern to the carving stock to reflect both the side view and the top view. Any shape, size, and detail presented by the outlines of both views will lend accuracy to the sawn out blank and greatly benefit in the carving sequences. Make sure that both pattern views are registered properly from top to bottom and from side to side.

Always begin a cane project such as this with an *accurately squared* block of wood stock. Cut the block to a size that will fit the pattern you have selected with just a bit to spare. A squared block is necessary to accurately drill the shaft or hardware receiving hole.

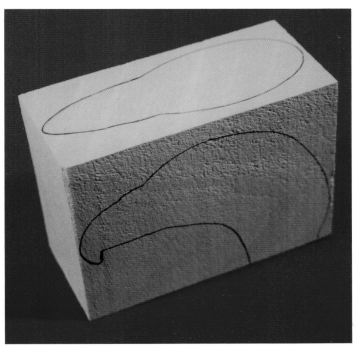

2. Make sure the top view and the side view are registered accurately one to the other. This is necessary for two reasons – first, to accurately saw the carving blank, and second, to accurately locate and drill the receiving hole for the shaft or cane hardware.

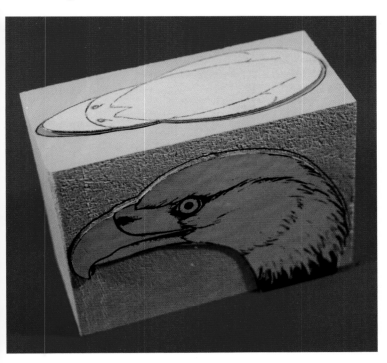

1. Transfer the outline of the side and top views of the pattern to the carving block by drawing around the patterns. (Make a template by gluing the pattern views to a piece of poster board or sheet plastic and carefully cutting them out.) I prefer this method because I can use the pattern template over and over again. Some carvers just make an extra copy of the pattern, cut out the outline, glue the views to the block with a glue stick, and then cut around the glued outline. This works if you don't plan to carve the same piece again. I prefer to keep the template patterns to use again or to share with students and carving friends.
The types of wood used for projects shown in the carving sequences for this book were milled Tupelo for the Bald Eagle, milled Walnut for the Mallard Duck, and a Red Maple tree for the Flamingo limb/trunk blank.

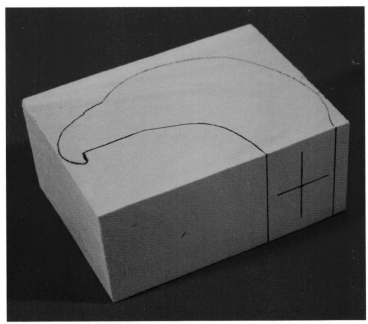

3. From the side view, transfer the thickness of the neck across the bottom of the carving block. Carefully measure and mark the centers along the length and width of the thickness of neck.

4. Choose the size of drill bit to create the receiving hole that will receive the cane shaft or cane hardware.

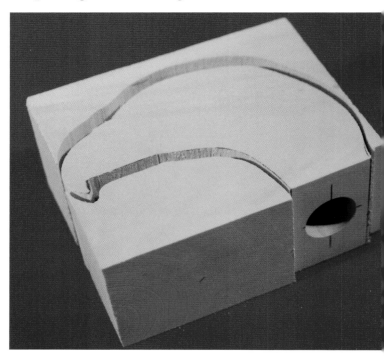

6. Cut the first view (the side view is usually best to start with) leaving the top and the bottom of the carving block intact. This not only preserves the outline of the top view for cutting, but also leaves support under the blank as it is being cut from the top.

5. Carefully register the drill bit on the center point of the receiving hole and drill the hole.

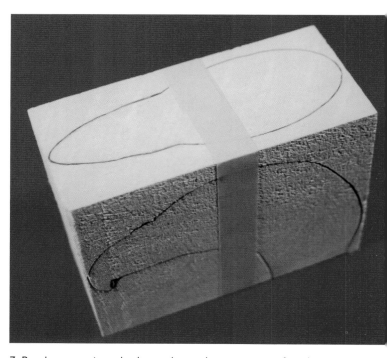

7. Put the sawn pieces back together and wrap a piece of masking tape around the entire assembly.

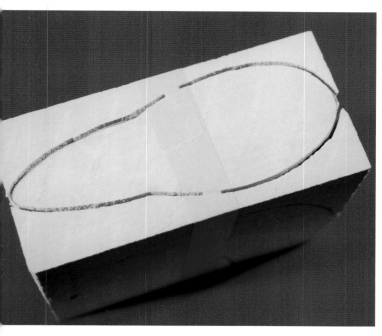

8. Saw the top view, leaving a portion of the masking tape to hold the pieces together where the tape has been wrapped across the top view.

9. Holding the blank with fingers away from the saw blade, finish cutting through the masking tape on both sides of the top view. Discard waste pieces.

Rough Carving the Blank

When roughing out, always be aware of the amount of stock that you are removing – leaving more is better. You can always remove stock as you go . . . it is tough to replace if you remove too much.

As the head is being rounded out, keep in mind the shape of the egg that the bird came from – no flat areas and no "squarish" corners.

1. Draw a centerline all around the carving blank, beginning at the tip of the beak and running through the beak, up over the head, down the center of the back of the neck and back to the point of beginning. Whenever the centerline is removed by the carving process, replace it, as it is extremely important to maintain symmetry while carving.

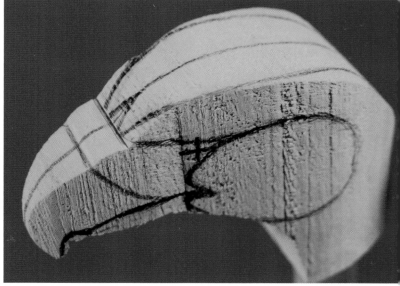

2. Draw all the detail control lines for the contours of the head – this will include the brow lines, the upper & lower mandibles (beaks), eye locations, and the cere (the thick soft section on the upper beak next to the forehead that surrounds the nostrils). Draw the auricular area, (the auricular area is often referred to as the cheek, but is actually the area of the ear hole that is covered by feathers), jowls, and throat feathers that run up on the bottom of the beak.

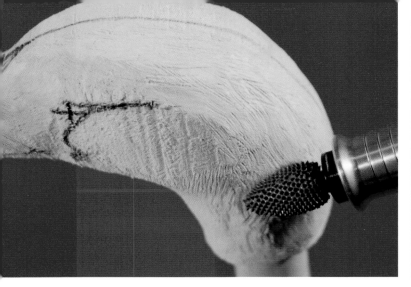

3. Using a medium sized flame shape carbide bit, round the top of the head down to the back of the neck. Round and shape the front and sides of the neck below the jowls and auricular area.

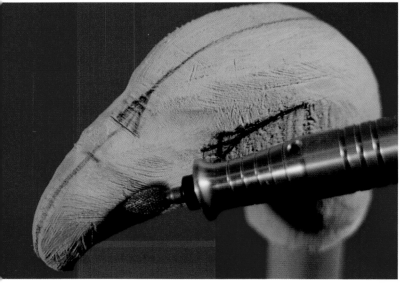

4. With a small flame shape carbide bit, rough shape the upper and lower beak. Leave extra stock.

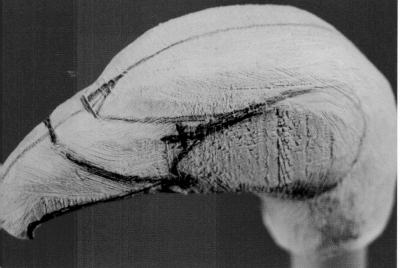

5. Replace centerline and area control lines as they were drawn in step two.

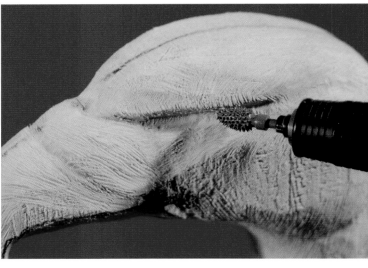

6. With a shallow cut, relieve away the groove for the eye valley beneath the brows. Remove just enough stock to allow the eye valley depression to be shaped. Check continuously from the front as you are carving to ensure that the eye valleys are symmetrical and evenly carved from side to side and from front to back.

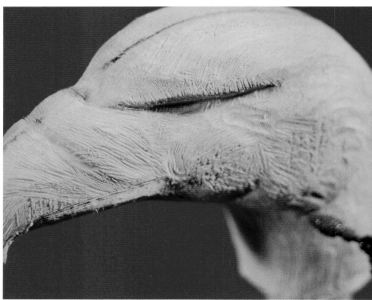

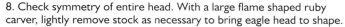

7. Shape contours of jowls and auricular (cheek) areas.

8. Check symmetry of entire head. With a large flame shaped ruby carver, lightly remove stock as necessary to bring eagle head to shape.

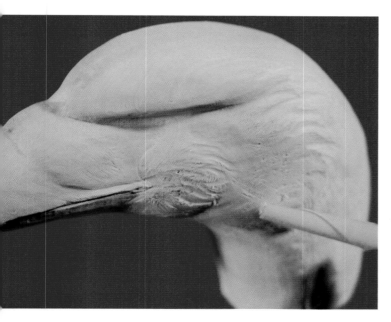

9. Lightly sand with a tapered mandrel to remove rough spots in preparation for refining and finishing detail.

Finish Carving and Detailing

Details for the eagle head will include finishing the beak, which will include the cere and nostrils. It should be noted that the beak has been drawn wider, and left wider on the carving than it would be on a natural eagle . . . the reason for this being to provide a larger, stronger handhold for the cane head.

Further finish shaping will include the remainder of the head such as the brows, jowls, and auricular area, and, finally, the layout of feather groups and feathers in preparation for texturing.

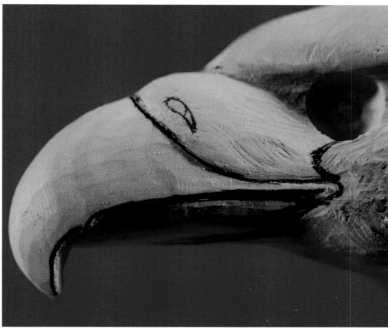

1. Draw the final shape of the break between the upper beak (upper mandible) and the lower beak (lower mandible). From a reference photo, note the sharpness and shape of the tip of the upper beak. Be sure to include the sickle or cutting edge just behind the tip of the beak. Observe where the separation between the upper and lower beak ends below the center of the eyes. Make very sure that the lines are the same length and symmetrical on both sides of the beak! Draw the extremes of the cere and the inner and outer shapes of the nostrils.

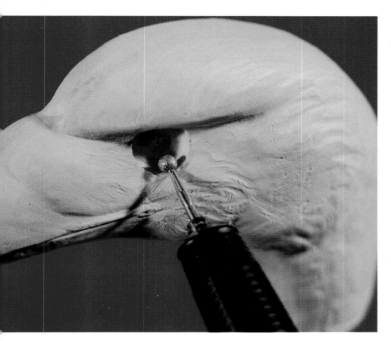

10. Prepare the eye areas for your choice of eyes – if glass eyes are preferred, cut in eye cavities with a ball shaped ruby carver in preparation to set eyes. Set eyes as described in the "Setting Glass Eyes" section on page 34; however, if carved eyes are preferred, carve the eyes as described in the "Carving Eyes" section on page 36.

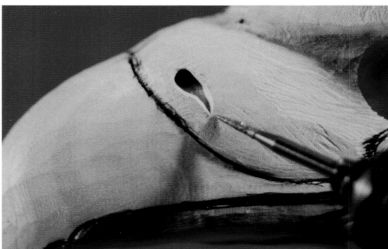

2. With a small flame shaped diamond bit, carve the nostrils to shape and desired depth.

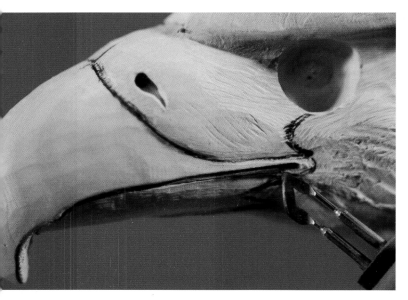

3. With a skew shaped wood burning tip, carefully burn in the separation line between the upper and lower beak. Before burning, again make very sure that the separation lines are drawn symmetrically on both sides of the beak.

4. Finish shaping the jowls and auricular patches on both sides of the head with a small tapered steel bit. Rough in a few feather lines in preparation for feather shaping and texturing.

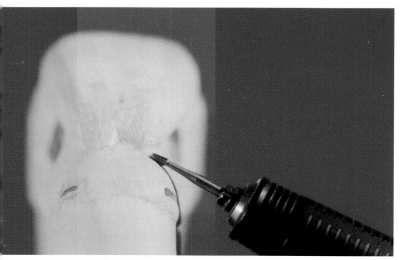

5. Finish shaping the feathers that run from the forehead onto the cere. Note the "V" shape that is formed as the feathers come onto the top of the cere and separate.

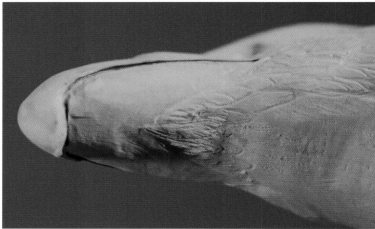

6. Finish shaping the group of feathers that run from the throat onto the underside of the beak to form a "V" shape.

7. Draw representative feathers on all feathered areas of the head. First, draw lines in the direction the feathers are to run over the entire head. While honoring the flow lines, draw feathers of the appropriate size over the entire head. Note that the feathers on the eagle's head are elongated and pointed. Shape as desired, and as described in the "Shaping Feathers" section on page 39.

8. Texture feathers as described in the "Texturing Feathers with a Stone Bit" section on page 41 or the "Texturing Feathers with a Wood Burner" section on page 42. The texturing illustrated was done with a medium sized inverted stone bit.

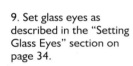

9. Set glass eyes as described in the "Setting Glass Eyes" section on page 34.

10. Clean the entire carving with a rotary brush to remove any and all debris left by the carving and/or wood burning process. Use care as any particles of dust will be sealed to the carving and are sure to show up during the painting process.

See "*Painting the Bald Eagle*" under Finishes, beginning on page 49.

Project Two
Carving the Mallard Duck

Prepare the carving blank as per directions in "Preparing the Carving Block" on page 23, and "Preparing the Carving Blank" on page 24. For this project, we will be using one-inch brass joining plates featured in "Hardware and Accessories" on page 16. Drill the receiving hole to accept this hardware.

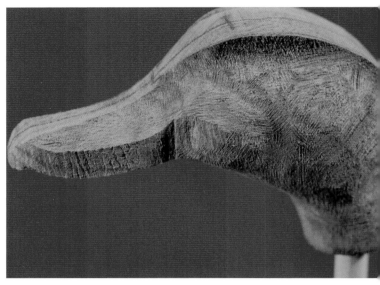

3. Round out the jowls, cheeks, and neck with a medium flame shaped carbide bit.

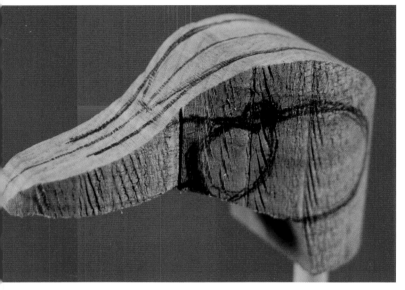

1. Draw a centerline all the way around the blank from top to bottom. Locate and draw eye centers, jowl & auricular (cheek) areas, and the thickness and shape of the top of head as it runs down to the ridge of the bill.

4. Draw detail of underside of beak. Note that feathers from the neck end in a "V" shape at the beginning of the beak.

5. Rough shape the beak with a small carbide bit, then blend brow, jowls, and throat feathers into beak with a large flame shape ruby carver.

2. With a large flame shaped carbide bit, outline the jowls, cheeks, and eye valleys. Remove "squareness" from the upper corners of the beak.

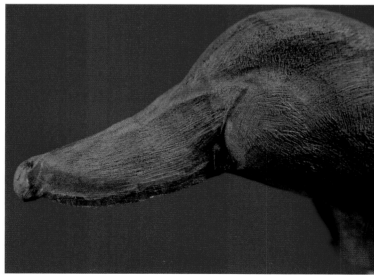

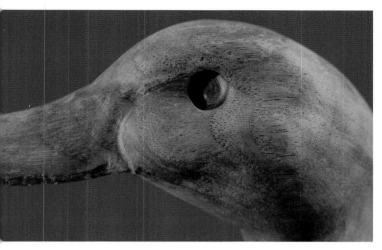

6. Locate eyes and carve eye cavities with a ball shaped ruby carver.

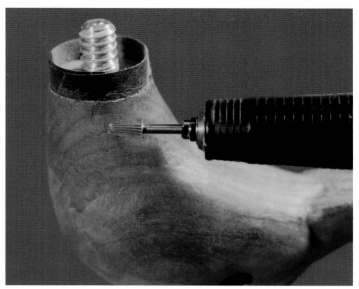

9. With a large tapered steel bit, remove the excess stock from around the joiner plate.

7. Glue one half of the joiner plate into the receiving hole of neck with epoxy glue. Use care not to allow excess glue to spread onto the plate or threads.

10. Texture the area around the base of the neck where the neck meets the joiner plate. Note where the inverted cone texturing bit has nicked the tape, but left no mark on the edge of the brass plate.

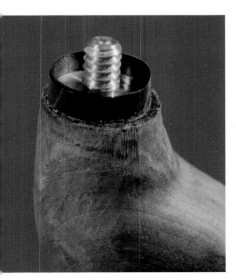

8. After epoxy glue sets, carefully wrap a piece of plastic electrician's tape around the plate of the joiner where it meets the bottom of the neck. The tape is to protect the edge of the joiner plate from being nicked or marred by the bit as the excess stock surrounding the joiner plate is carved away.

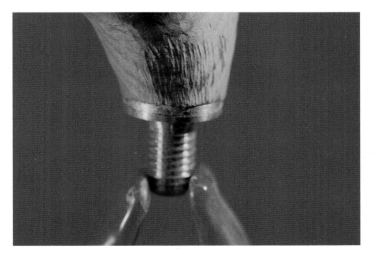

11. Texture to a safe distance away from the disc and bottom of the neck, remove tape, and clean with a rotary brush.

12. Draw "flow" lines over the entire head to indicate the direction the hair-like feathers on the head will take.

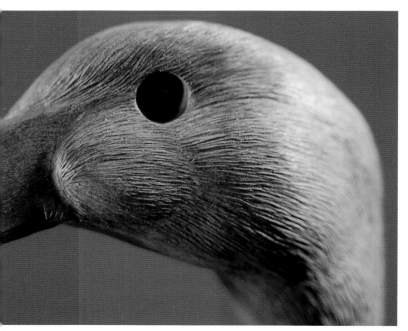

13. Texture entire head with a medium to large inverted cone shaped stone bit.

14. Draw nostrils, front ridge of beak, and separation of upper and lower beak.

15. With a small flame shaped diamond bit, cut in and shape the nostril. With a medium-small tapered steel bit, carve the front beak ridges back from the egg hook on the front of the beak. Separate the upper and lower beak from one another with a skew shaped wood burning pen, then shape the division as necessary with a small flame shaped diamond bit.

16. To bed the eye and model the eyelids, I use Quikwood® epoxy wood repair putty. This material gives sufficient time to model eyes within about 30 minutes. If you anticipate using more time than this, mix enough to do only one eye at a time. I prefer Quikwood to bed eyes on carvings where I want a natural finish, because it readily accepts wood stains that will match the wood color I have used.

17. Install eyes, using care to achieve symmetry from side to side, top to bottom, and from front to rear.

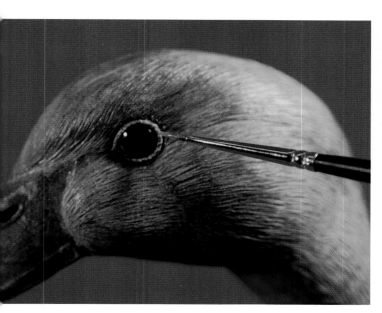

18. Stain eyelids with a stain that matches the wood used for the carving – in this case, *Special Walnut* by the Minwax® Company.

20. Apply a natural stain finish to enhance the wood grain and seal the carving. The Minwax® Company manufactures a very satisfactory natural stain. Allow it to dry for 24 hours.

19. Finish the detail on the underside of the beak by outlining the details with a small ball shaped diamond bit, and blending with a small flame shaped ruby carver. Cut in "teeth" on the exposed bottom of the upper mandible near the front with a small flame shaped diamond bit.

21. Complete the carving with one or more coats of a good exterior polyurethane finish.

33

Glass Eyes

I prefer setting glass eyes in my carvings of birds, especially for cane heads, because I feel it gives the carving as well as the cane a more realistic, finished, and attractive look. For example, I like the looks of an eagle cane head carved from black walnut with yellow glass eyes. The whole cane head seems to come alive because more realism can be given to a carving with glass eyes and modeled eyelids, than can be given to a carved eye, with much less time and effort. Glass eyes are preferred for several reasons, but the primary reasons are realism and ease of setting. Other reasons include uniformity of size and roundness, color, and shine.

There are many carvers who would prefer to carve eyes rather than set glass eyes and for them I have included a section on carving eyes (see *Carving Eyes*).

Setting Glass Eyes

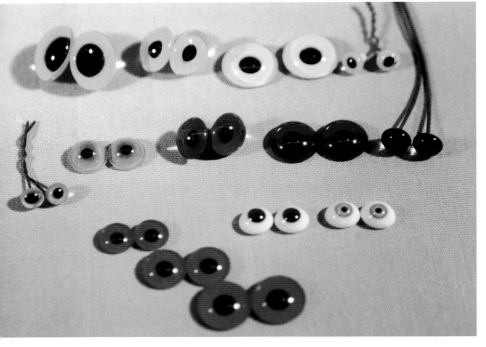

1. Select proper size and color of eyes for the project.

2. Ensure that the eye locations are perfectly drawn from side to side, and that they are symmetrical and even when viewed from the front, top, and sides. Nothing will ruin the appearance of the carving more than eyes that are poorly located, with one eye higher than the other, or one further back on the head than the other. It is imperative that the surface immediately around the eye be relieved enough to allow the eye to be inserted and plumb. (The flat back of the eye must be straight up and down as opposed to be tilted in or out.) Take the time to check position from all possible directions, and adjust as necessary. This is the time to take steps to correct any imperfections, rather than trying to make adjustments later on.

3. Using a ball shaped bit, touch the bit to the center of the eye location, and begin applying pressure without letting the bit wander. Using a slight circular motion, begin shaping the eye hole until the shape of the hole is of proper depth and diameter to fit the eye. As you approach the size of the eye, keep fitting the eye to the hole until the eye will slide into the hole.

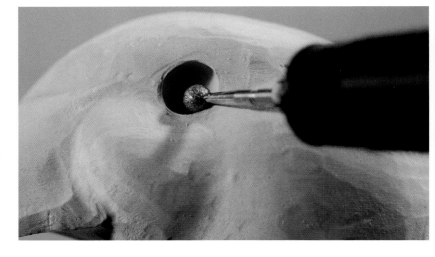

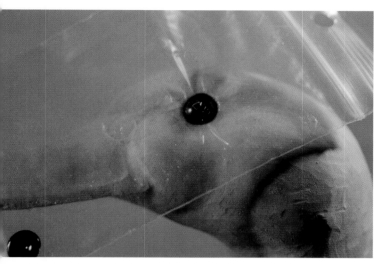

6. Before you start the glass eye installation, you should have a modeling tool. This tool will be used to properly position the eye as it is being pushed into the eye cavity, remove excess epoxy, to model the shape of the eye, and to model and texture the eyelids. The simplest and most effective tool is a ¼-inch dowel that has been sharply tapered at one end and semi-sharpened with a concave indentation at the other.

4. Leave the eyes in a plastic bag and fit an eye to the hole through the bag. When the eye and the thickness of the bag will enter the hole, the hole is of the proper size.

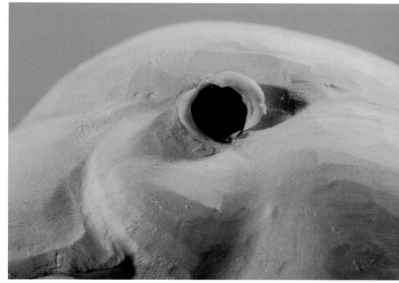

7. Push the eye into the eye cavity with the tip of the dowel modeling tool having the concave indentation. Push until the eye protrudes out of the head by the desired amount. Hint: A general rule of thumb is to allow the eye to extend out of the head by approximately one-third of the eye's diameter.

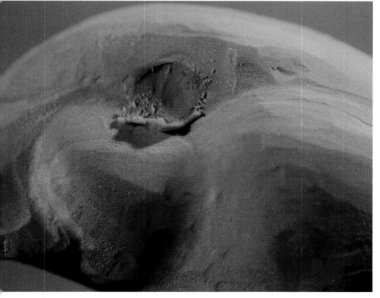

5. Fill the eye cavity with two part epoxy putty (not the five minute variety!) and level to the edges of the cavity.

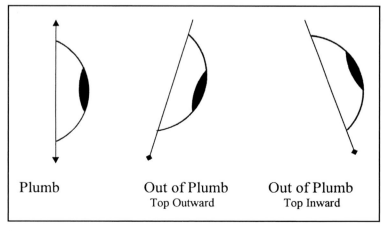

Plumb   Out of Plumb
Top Outward   Out of Plumb
Top Inward

8. Make sure the eye is plumb with respect to the bird's head. An easy way to check this is to think of the back of the eye as a flat plain and make sure that the flat is straight up and down and not tilted outward or inward within the eye cavity.

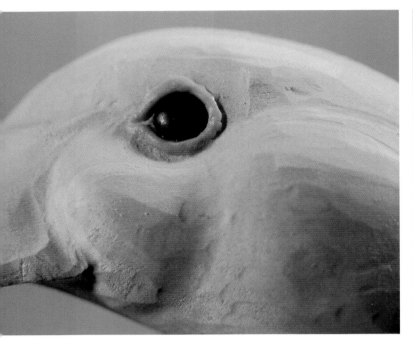

9. Remove excess epoxy putty that is pushed out of the cavity as the eye displaces it, and model an eyelid of the type that is suitable to the type of bird being carved. Hint: Gather whatever reference photos you can featuring the eye area of the bird that you are carving.

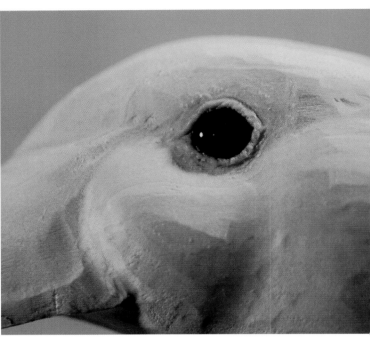

11. After the epoxy has set, clean any film and/or residue of the eye by rubbing the tip of the modeling tool around and around on the surface of the eye, within the eyelids. This will make the eye shiny and unblemished, as it should be.

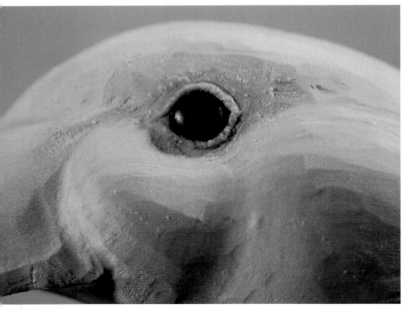

10. Touch up each eye to assure that the eyes match as closely as possible. Do not handle the carving until the epoxy putty has thoroughly hardened. Hint: In order to ascertain that the modeled epoxy around the eye has hardened, make a small ball of leftover epoxy from the same batch as used on the eye and test it from time to time to see when proper hardness is achieved.

Carving Eyes

Due to the ease of installation, preference is usually given to setting *glass* eyes on bird carvings; however, on functional carvings such as cane heads or walking sticks, some carvers prefer to carve the eyes rather than setting glass eyes. In fact, some carvers prefer the carved effect throughout their carvings. For them, we include the eye carving sequence that follows.

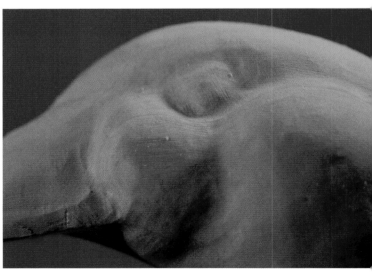

1. Prepare both sides of the head where the eyes will be located uniformly – ensure that there is a slight mound from which to carve the eye, and that the mound blends back into the eye valley as it would on the real bird.

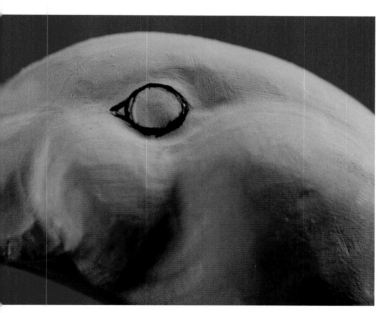

2. Draw the proper size and shape of each eye on the eye mounds, making certain that they are symmetrical and that each eye is properly located to the other from top to bottom and from front to back (a badly located or out of place eye will ruin the look of the whole carving).

4. Another excellent method to outline and cut an eye is with a bullet casing. The casing shown in the hand drill chuck is a 357 Magnum that I picked up from a firing range. I grind the ridge down to the body of the casing, notch it on either side, and I have a ready-made eye bit. The wall of the casing has sufficient strength to be held by the fingers of the chuck without collapsing. I apply just enough pressure when I put the casing in the chuck to be assured that the casing is securely held.

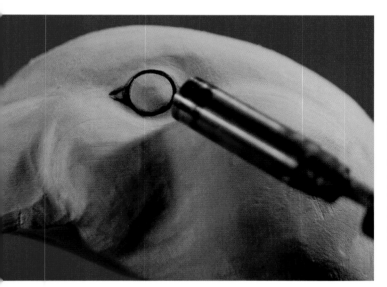

3. The easiest way to cut in a round eye is with a piece of brass tube of the proper size, mounted on a hand drill. File a small notch or two on the cutting end of the tube so it will more readily cut and require less pressure. Brass tubing can be obtained from most hardware or hobby supply stores. Shown is a homemade eye bit produced from silver soldering stacked tubing and a 1/8-inch brass welding rod for a bit shaft.

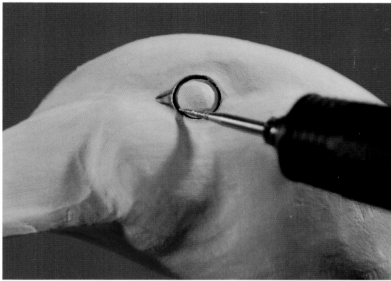

5. Using a small flame shaped diamond bit, round the outline of the eye into a uniform sphere.

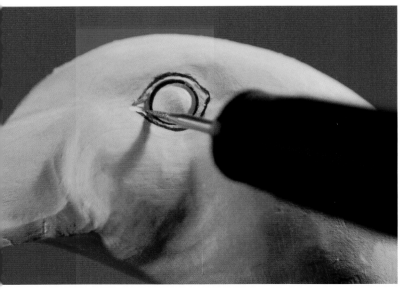

6. Using a small flame shaped diamond bit with a fine grit, cut the "V" shape hollow leading back to the front of the eye.

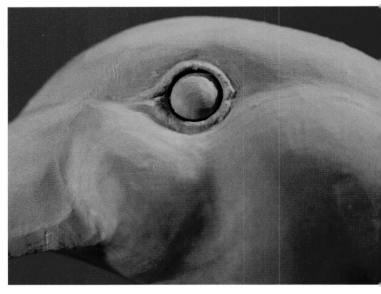

8. Smooth the eye and lids as necessary, and seal with clear lacquer.

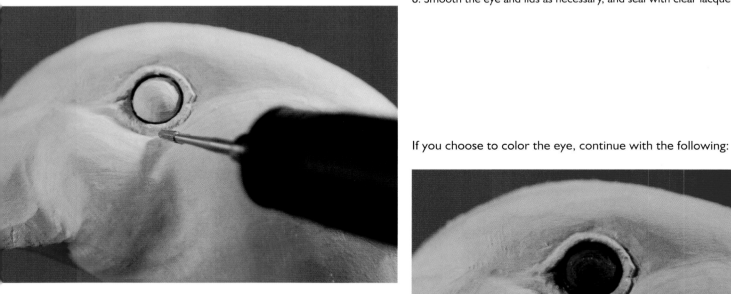

7. Shape the surrounding eyelids away from the eye with a small ball shaped diamond bit, then shape/blend the outer edges of the lids back into the head with a small flame shaped diamond bit. Lid shapes will vary from bird to bird, so study photographic references or the real bird.

If you choose to color the eye, continue with the following:

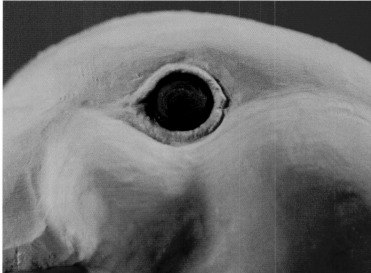

9. Apply eye color.

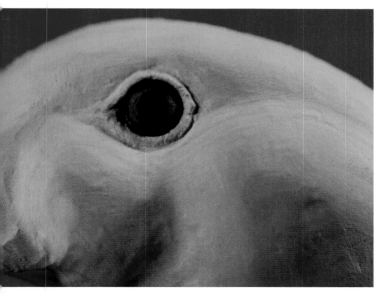

10. Apply pupil. Depending on the size of the pupil desired, the rounded end of a dowel or an old paintbrush handle works nicely when touched to a puddle of black paint on the palette, and then touched carefully to the center of the eye dome. Practice before trying this on the carving – you need the right consistency of paint so it won't run, and the right depth of paint on the palette to give the right pupil size.

Feathers

For purpose of description within this book, *contour feathers* (breast, coverts, rump, nape, neck, and head) will be considered as those feathers that provide protection, warmth, and have a softer look about them than do flight feathers. *Flight feathers* (wing, tail, tertiary, and scapular feathers) will be considered as those feathers that sustain flight and have a flatter, harder look.

For the above considerations, I prefer to create contour feathers by relieving/shaping with a steel bit, and texturing with a stone bit, which gives them a softer look than the flight feathers, which I relieve away with a bent wood burner, then texture with a sharp skew burner.

Some carvers prefer to texture the entire bird by wood burning. For them, I would recommend the combination of shaping contour feathers with a steel bit, shaping flight feathers with a bent wood burning skew pen as usual, then texturing the entire bird with a wood burner as is their preference.

Shaping Feathers

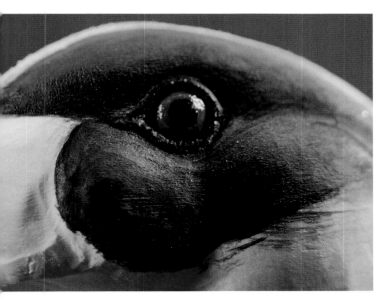

11. Carefully apply several coats of gloss lacquer over the dome shape of the eye and allow to dry thoroughly.

1. Draw feathers of the appropriate shape and scale for the size of bird being carved.

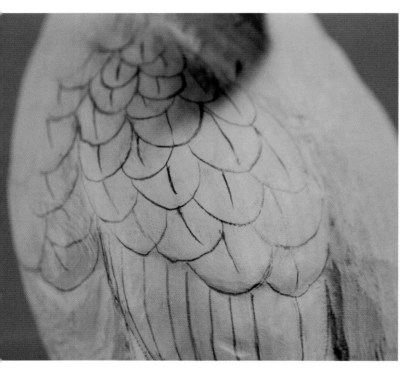

2. Draw "flow" lines to exemplify the bend of individual feathers as well as the direction of the feather group as a whole. This will be of great aid not only when shaping, but also when texturing the feathers. These lines are not to be carved as separate quills (main feather stems) as they are drawn to indicate direction to *aid the carver*.

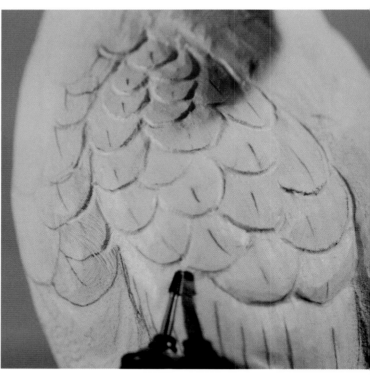

4. Using the flat portion of the bit, flatten and smooth out around the *outside* of each feather. It is usually easier and more convenient to start with the rearmost feathers and work forward.

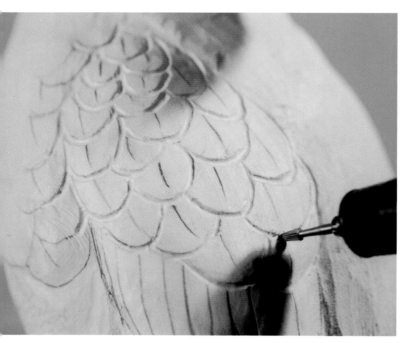

3. Using an appropriately sized tapered steel fluted bit, *outline* each feather using the tip of the bit with the hand piece held at approximately 45-degrees.

5. Using the flat portion of the bit, round up and shape each outlined feather. Think of the rounded shape of a clamshell for each feather, rather than a shingle that drops off sharply.

6. Redraw any lost flow lines. With a small flame shaped diamond bit, accentuate the feathers by cutting voids between feathers that look pressed together and undercut the occasional feather slightly to give it the appearance of being raised away from the surface of the carving.

7. It helps to outline feathers lightly with a pencil to make feathers highly visible in preparation for pre-texturing and texturing.

Texturing Feathers with a Stone Bit

8. With a stone ball bit of appropriate size to the feathers being textured, cut a sunburst pattern that follows the line that the *barbules** of a feather would take. Pre-texturing with a ball in this manner gives the feather a softer, fuller, and more realistic look after final texturing. **Barbules* are those hair-like veins that come off the center portion or quill of the feather and determine the overall shape of the feather.

9. With an inverted cone or cylinder shaped stone bit of appropriate size, texture each feather following the shape dictated by the pre-texturing lines or the penciled flow lines. *Rule: Always texture from the rear forward, and from the bottom to the top of the feather groups.*

10. When all feathers are completely textured, clean entire feathered area with a rotary brush run at a slow to medium speed. It is imperative that the texturing debris be removed from the textured area. If a rotary brush is not available, use an old toothbrush and scrub the textured feathers clean. Any tiny particles left on the carving from the texturing operation will be locked on the surface when the carving is sealed in preparation for the final finish, so be thorough with the cleaning process.

Texturing Feathers with a Wood Burner

Texturing Contour Feathers

1. With a stone ball bit of appropriate size, cut a sunburst pattern that follows the line that the *barbules** of a feather would take. Pre-texturing with a ball in this manner gives the feather a softer, fuller, and more realistic look after final texturing.

2. With a skew shaped wood burner, texture each feather following the shape dictated by the pre-texturing lines or the penciled flow lines. *Always texture from the rear forward, and from the bottom to the top of the feather groups.*

3. When all feathers are completely textured, clean the entire feathered area with a rotary brush run with a light touch at a slow to medium speed.

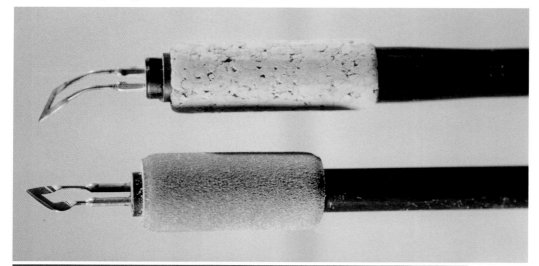

1. The two burning pens used for burning hard-surfaced flight feathers are the large straight skew pen, and the large bent skew blank. This is called a blank because the skewed edge of the pen is unsharpened as is a blank pen at the manufacturer's before it is sharpened and prepared for sale. When combined with the proper amount of heat, the dulled edges (sides and bottom) are necessary for relieving the feather(s) away and giving the feather group a realistic "stacked" look such as is found on a bird.

2. Draw feathers in place with a pencil. The area where the feathers are to be drawn should be sanded and smooth before feathers are drawn.

3. Outline feathers with the bent skew pen. I get better results when I relieve from the top feather down to the bottom feathers. Hold the pen flat, and maintain steady movement on each stroke. Steady movement is necessary to the uniform burning and outlining of the feathers.

4. Texture feathers with a large straight skew using measured strokes with an even heat. "Even heat" will depend on a heat setting that satisfies the type of stroke being used, the speed of stroke being used, and the type of wood being used. Start from the bottom and work up, and the rear working forward. *Hint: If you feel heavy friction with each stroke, chances are you are burning at too low a heat setting. If you don't feel **any** friction and the strokes appear dark and deep, chances are your heat setting is too high.*

5. Thoroughly clean the textured surface with a rotary brush. Be careful not to use too much pressure and too high a speed, or the brush will obliterate the texture.

Finishing

Cleaning – as previously stated, upon completion of the feather texturing process, whether stone grinding texture or wood burning texture, it is imperative that the carving be cleaned completely. I find the large soft-bristled rotary brush with a two-inch diameter ideal for cleaning any carving that I have done. The problem is that, at this point in time, I have not been able to find another one like it. The one shown I found in a Florida flea market. For the two years that I have had it, it has cleaned every carving to date. Unfortunately, I have not been able to find another like it. I have had to supply the students at my school with a similar rotary brush, only it measures one-inch in diameter instead of the preferable two-inch diameter brush.

For those without a rotary brush to clean debris from a carving, a soft toothbrush scrubbed and swept in the direction of the texture lines will suffice. Using the toothbrush will take longer and require much more effort.

Keep in mind that it is of absolute importance that the carving be as clean as possible before it is sealed! If any of the tiny bits of grinding dust from stone texturing or char dust from wood burner texturing are left on the surface of the carving and not removed, they will be locked in place forever when the sealer is applied. These lumps may not be readily visible upon the initial application of the sealer, but when gesso is applied, they will pull more gesso from the brush than the surrounding surface and each lump will become magnified. When the paint is applied, especially if applied with a manual brush, these troublesome lumps tend to enlarge even more, and will be quite noticeable when under either a strong light or natural sunlight.

The best and most unforgiving light that may be employed to check for existing dirt prior to sealing is morning sunlight. Not only will this type of light reveal dirt, but very often I find other things to correct on the carving. That's why I call it an unforgiving light – it seems to be relentless in its ability to reveal imperfections in a carving.

Sealing – I seal all of my carvings with acrylic automotive lacquer. Thin the lacquer with lacquer thinner at a ratio of *50% lacquer to 50% lacquer thinner*. I apply the thinner with a large natural bristle brush, and allow the carving to accept as much as possible without losing any texture detail. The deeper the sealer penetrates the better. I don't use a commercially prepared sanding sealer, due to problems I have had in the past with it filling and obliterating texture detail.

Paint – for *manual brush application*, it makes little difference what acrylic paint manufacturer you use, as long as that particular paint, its consistency, and range of colors satisfies you and complements the manner in which you apply color. If you are like most, it will take a while for you to "settle in" with the manufacturer of a paint that satisfies you the most. There is one that I consider too "slippery" as it comes off the brush and is blended – yet many of my fellow carvers swear by it. Another just feels too gritty and dry as it is blended and I just don't feel comfortable with it – yet it is preferred over all by other woodcarvers. There are even some reds and oranges by one manufacturer that I like better than another, yet I dislike their earth colors. Experience and use will establish a preference. I finally settled on the Grumbacher® and Liquitex® brands as those that best meet my needs during manual brush application.

For *airbrush* color application on woodcarvings, I use Holbein Aeroflash® liquid acrylic color. I used and experimented with several different brands of acrylic paints manufactured specifically for airbrushes and enjoyed only limited success. I was looking for smoothness and consistency in a pre-mixed liquid that I, as well as my students, could use over extended periods of time without clogging an airbrush or causing undue drying or crusting on the tips of the airbrushes. In short, I wanted the easiest to apply, most forgiving mixture of airbrush paint that I could find that would create the least problem whether being used by an individual or by a group in an instructional setting.

Stain — unless I actually have to, I use *only* a grain enhancer such as Minwax® Natural Stain (see *Carving the Mallard Duck*) to bring out the beauty of the grain in the carving to which I am applying finish.

If I have to use stain on bland woods such as Basswood, Tupelo, or Poplar, I add thin coats of stain until I get the depth of color that I want. I allow each coat to dry thoroughly before I add the next coat, which I feel gives me maximum penetration. If I am staining for a walnut finish, I stain until I get a surface that looks like walnut, instead of a basswood surface that looks like it has a coat of walnut stain over it.

Finish — There are many excellent finishes on the market with which to give a final and appealing protective coating to a cane or walking stick. Of the choices available, I have used deck enamel, marine varnishes, and polyurethanes in flat, matte, and gloss finishes. The new marine clear finishes have provided the best longevity when subjected to the roughest abuse over any given terrain. Most of the canes I have carved are finished with several thinned coats of a matte finish polyurethane which provides satisfactory finish for canes subjected to normal use.

Painting Materials and Techniques

Manual Brush

Only two types of brushes were used for the projects throughout this book. One was a round Kolinsky® sable brush and the other was a sable bristled Filbert® brush. Although the sizes of the brushes varied from project to project, the type of brush and quality remained the same.

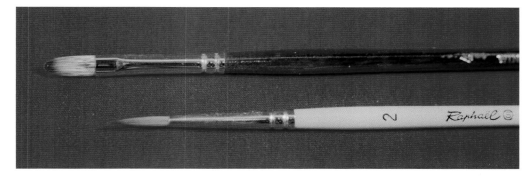

A round Kolinsky sable brush and a sable bristled Filbert brush.

There is an axiom about brushes that I have found to be true for the whole of my carving and painting career, and that is: Buy the best brush that you can afford. Nothing performs better than a quality brush, and if properly used, nothing seems to last longer than a quality brush.

I have found the Raphael® and Windsor-Newton® brushes to be the most to my liking, with the higher quality lines of Grumbacher® brushes also giving excellent results. A good brush should be cared for and treated with the attention that any fine tool should receive to ensure long-life.

Before I subject any of my brushes to the paint on my palette, I dunk them in the medium that I will be using to thin my paint. If it is oil paint, I first dunk the brush in turpentine, if it is acrylic paint, I first dunk the brush in water. I was once told by an art teacher to allow the ferrule to fill with the thinning medium first, which will keep pure paint from going into the ferrule and clogging it, which will eventually displace the bristles to the point that the brush will be deformed.

Brushes should be thoroughly cleaned and dried after use. I use a gentle sudsy mixture of washing liquid and warm water, then I rinse thoroughly with clean warm water. After partially drying, I reshape each brush with my lips, and store vertically (with the bristles up) in a container, or roll several brushes in a thick piece of cloth the size of a place mat and store horizontally.

As I use a brush, especially a round brush, I hold the manufacturer's name upward in my grip while I paint. This may seem odd, but I believe, through use, that the bristles become conditioned to being used in the same manner each time, and therefore perform in the same manner each time.

Airbrush

As with a manual brush, choose the best airbrush you can afford that not only performs, but gives the result you want with the least amount of effort. Current "MSRPs" (manufacturer suggested retail prices) run from around $25 to more than $575, so along with an extremely wide range of price, the beginning airbrusher has just as wide a range of quality, function, and performance to consider.

I have had the opportunity to use and evaluate a wide range of airbrushes (I believe I had 29 different airbrushes!) from every manufacturer in the United States and Canada. The reason for accumulating so many airbrushes was to provide material for an article that I wrote on airbrushes for the Fall 1999 issue of *Woodcarving Illustrated*, entitled, "Airbrushes for Woodcarvers."

That article generated more interest in airbrushes and learning to airbrush than I could believe, so much so that I decided to incorporate completely outfitted painting stations, each complete with an airbrush and accessories at my woodcarving school in Vermont.

I pushed all the airbrushes featured in that article to every extreme that I could think of just to see how one compared to the other or how each compared to the whole lot. For the type of painting applications that I use myself and intended to teach, I ended up completely sold on three airbrushes, each a different model by a different airbrush manufacturer. The one with the highest quality with respect to construction, facility of use, durability, and ease of maintenance, was the model that I decided to install at each position at the school.

For the use and abuse that they receive at the school, the Holbein model Y-2 Dash® airbrushes have continued to function without mechanical problems ever since we began using them two years ago. The only time I have had a performance problem with any brush is when a student is lax about cleaning, and that usually doesn't take too long to remedy.

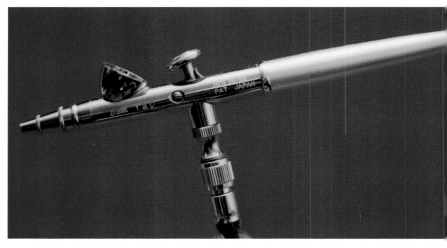

2. the Holbein model Y-2 Dash airbrushes . . .

The greatest problem encountered with any airbrush stems from not keeping the airbrush properly cleaned. Hopefully, the airbrush you are using is of the highest quality available to you. If so, that airbrush should continue to serve you well as long as it is kept clean.

At first, cleaning between color changes may seem to be a chore, but soon it will become so much a part of the painting routine that it is done automatically and with little thought.

If you ever have cause to use an airbrush that has been improperly cared for, you will soon realize and appreciate why cleaning an airbrush should be a second-nature action.

The model Y-2 Dash airbrush is manufactured by:

H.K. Holbein, Inc.
Box 555
20 Commerce Street
Williston, Vermont 05495

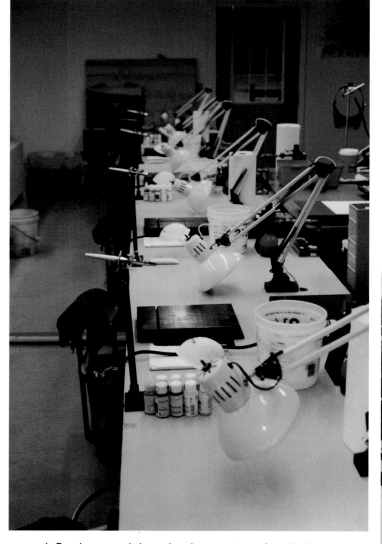

1. For the use and abuse that they receive at the school, . . .

3. have continued to function without mechanical problems ever since we began using them two years ago. *Thanks to student Ginette Drolet of Quebec, Canada.*

Color Change Cleansing

Clean the airbrush every time you change color in the following manner:

Remove as much of the color being used as possible from the color cup on the airbrush. Either pour it back into the container, or dispose of it if only a small amount remains.

Fill the color cup with water from a cleansing bowl, and swirl the color cup with a brush to loosen paint on the sides of the cup.

Shoot dirty water into a waste barrel for a bit, then dump the remainder into the waste barrel.

Immerse the tip of the airbrush into the cleansing bowl and hold the tip of your finger over the tip of the airbrush while holding the airbrush full open for both color flow and air. This is called *backflushing*, and probably does more to keep the airbrush passage clear than any other operation.

Now spray a few squirts of airbrush cleaner (Windex®) into the color cup and then spray the airbrush into the waste barrel.

While spraying cleaner, place your finger tip over the airbrush tip and backflush, then remove your finger and allow the cleaner to flow forward. Do this once or twice.

Rinse the airbrush in a clean water bowl, and add new color.

Shoot into a waste barrel until pure color is observed.

Final Cleaning

When you have finished with the airbrush, thoroughly clean the airbrush internally as detailed above. Once you are satisfied that the airbrush is completely clean on the inside, dampen a paper towel or a soft cloth with airbrush cleaner (Windex®). With the exception of the tip, carefully wipe all external surfaces of the airbrush to remove any surface paint that may be apparent – especially around the color cup.

Check the tip to ascertain how much paint may remain on the tip surrounding the needle.

If there appears to be only a small amount of paint residue, wad the cloth or paper towel into a small ball, spray it with airbrush cleaner, and CAREFULLY push the tip of the airbrush against the wad while rotating the airbrush.

If there appears to be a fairly large amount of paint residue, squeeze the end of a flat tipped bristle brush together, soak with airbrush cleaner and carefully place tip of the airbrush against the tips of the bristles and rotate.

Once the tip of the airbrush is clean and dry, *replace the metal airbrush tip cover* and wipe the entire airbrush with a water-dampened cloth.

Wipe the entire airbrush with a dry cloth and secure the airbrush.

Applying Color

To maintain control over the color, whether it is being applied with a manual brush or an airbrush, it should be applied in thin layers.

When applying color with a manual brush, it should never be applied directly from the tube, but should be mixed with an appropriate thinning medium (i.e.: water for acrylics, turpentine for oils) so as to provide an even, controllable coat of color. It may take several washes of color (for acrylics) to attain the depth and tone of color desired. For example, by applying washes of color, the depth of color can be brought up to a certain level by using darker shades or it can be brought down by using lighter shades of the same color.

Painting the Bald Eagle

1. Seal the carving completely with clear matte finish acrylic automotive lacquer or Deft® matte finish. Thin the lacquer or Deft 50/50 with lacquer thinner. Allow the carving to absorb all the thinned lacquer it will take.

2. Gesso the entire carving with several coats of thinned gesso. I prefer to apply gesso with a stiff bristle brush using a scrubbing motion that forces the gesso particles into the detail of the carving. The gesso should be of a coffee-cream consistency, which will allow the color of the wood to show through on the first coat. Apply thin coats until the entire surface of the carving is an opaque white. *Note: I paint over glass eyes during the entire seal, gesso, and color application process for two reasons. First, it saves time; secondly, it gives me freedom and a better sense of continuation for painting lines and/or shadows through the eyes — without having to stop from one side of the eye to the other.*

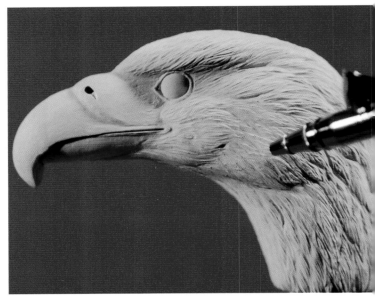

4. Spread a mixture of Titanium White with much less Burnt Umber than was used in the previous step over the rest of the white feathered areas of the head.

3. Apply a mixture of Titanium White with a touch of Burnt Umber as the shade color to all deepened areas of the carving that would normally appear darker. Color should be heavier in the crevices and thin out to nothing as it approaches the high points.

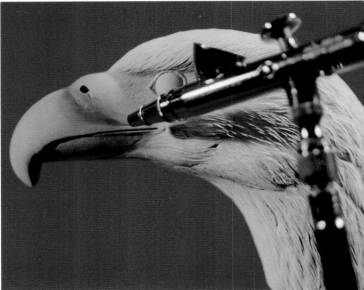

5. Use a mixture of Yellow Ochre and a touch of Raw Umber to create the darkened and shaded areas of the beak.

6. Finish the lighter areas of the beak with Yellow Ochre with a touch of Cadmium Yellow (medium).

8. Finish the color application by highlighting different feathers and feather details with Titanium White and a round brush.

9. Remove paint from the eyes by outlining them with an Xacto® or pointed scalpel-type blade. Cut around the inside of the eyelid with the point, then cut around the eye with the flat of the blade. Finish cleaning the residue with the dowel modeling tool that was used to set the eye. Paint the black inner ring of the eye and re-clean the eye.

7. Wash the entire head with a *very* thin mixture of Raw Umber and water, allowing the mixture to flow into the deeper details of the carving, but not on the higher details. This will accentuate the feather and texture detail.

10. Complete the carving with a protective covering of one or more coats of matte or flat finish lacquer or polyurethane.

Carving Projects

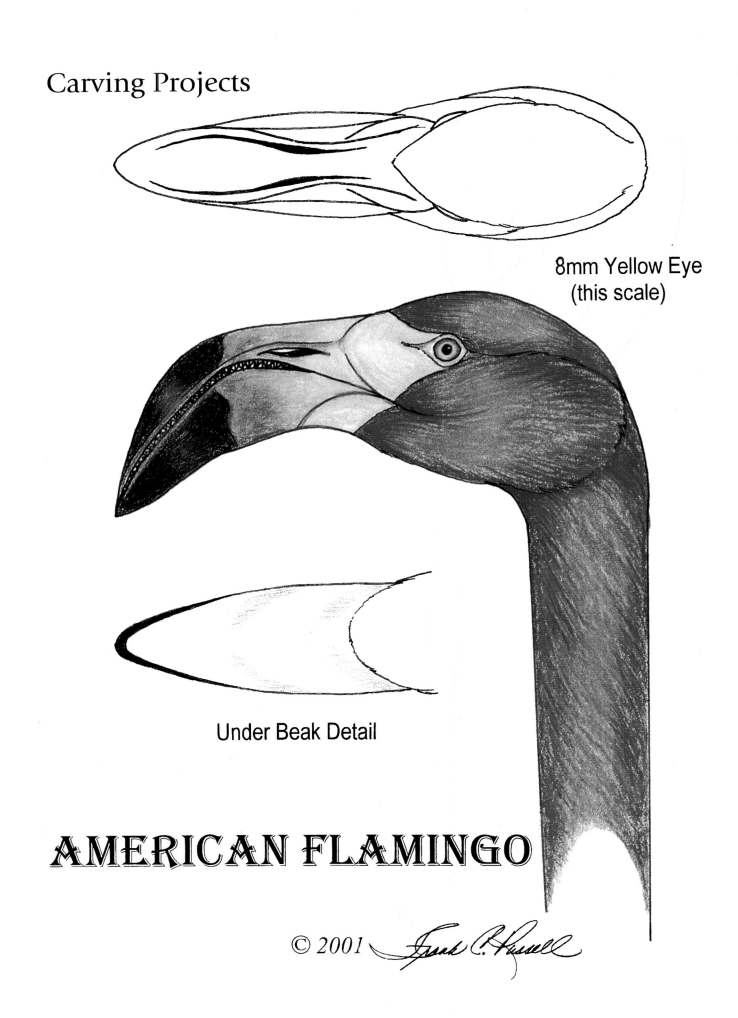

8mm Yellow Eye
(this scale)

Under Beak Detail

AMERICAN FLAMINGO

© 2001 *Frank C. Russell*

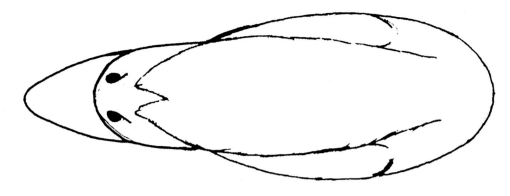

12mm Yellow Eye
(this scale)

Under Beak Detail

BALD EAGLE

© 2001 Frank C. Russell

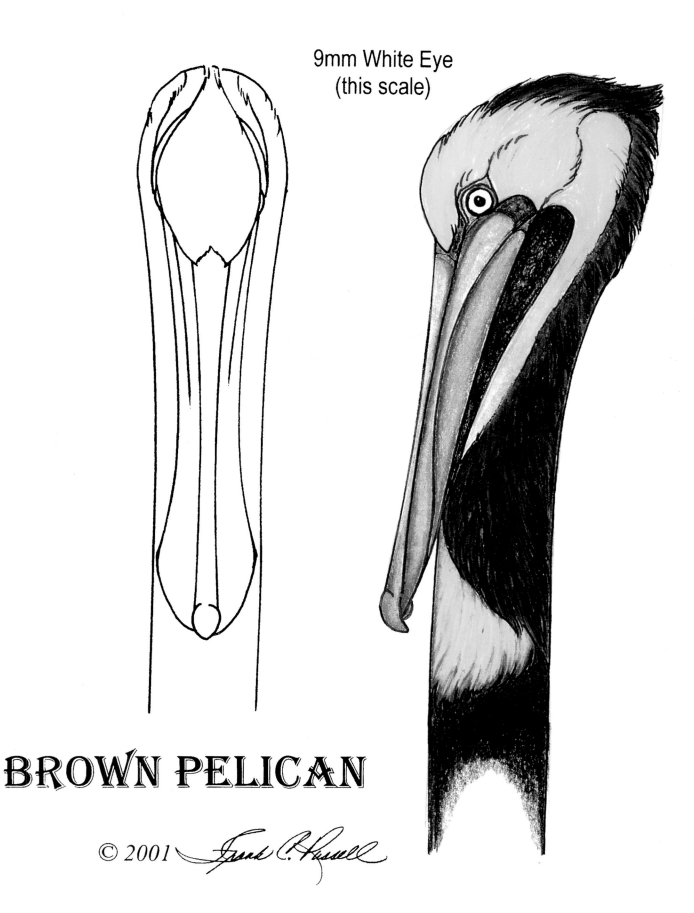

9mm White Eye
(this scale)

BROWN PELICAN

© 2001 Frank C. Russell

CARDINAL

7mm Brown Eye
(this scale)

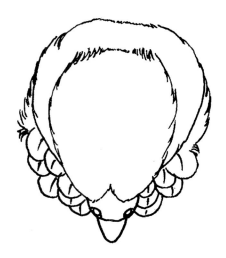

10mm Red Eye
(this scale)

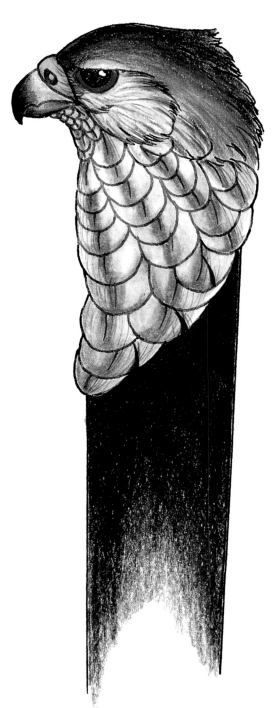

COOPER'S HAWK

© 2001 *Frank C. Russell*

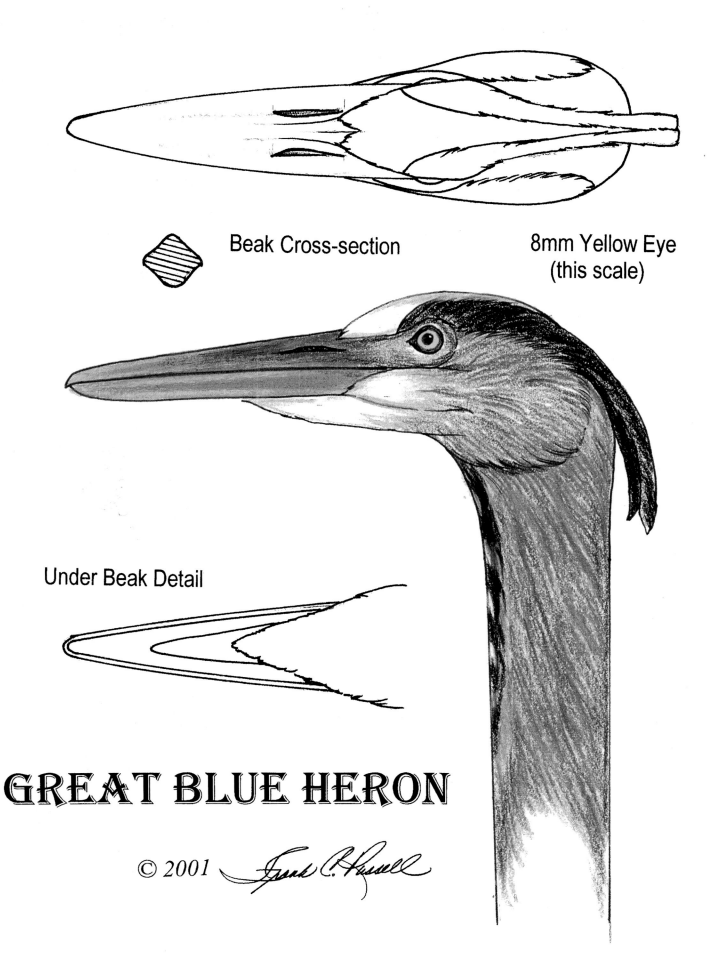

Beak Cross-section

8mm Yellow Eye
(this scale)

Under Beak Detail

GREAT BLUE HERON

© 2001 *Frank C. Russell*

HORNED PUFFIN

© 2001 *Frank C. Russell*

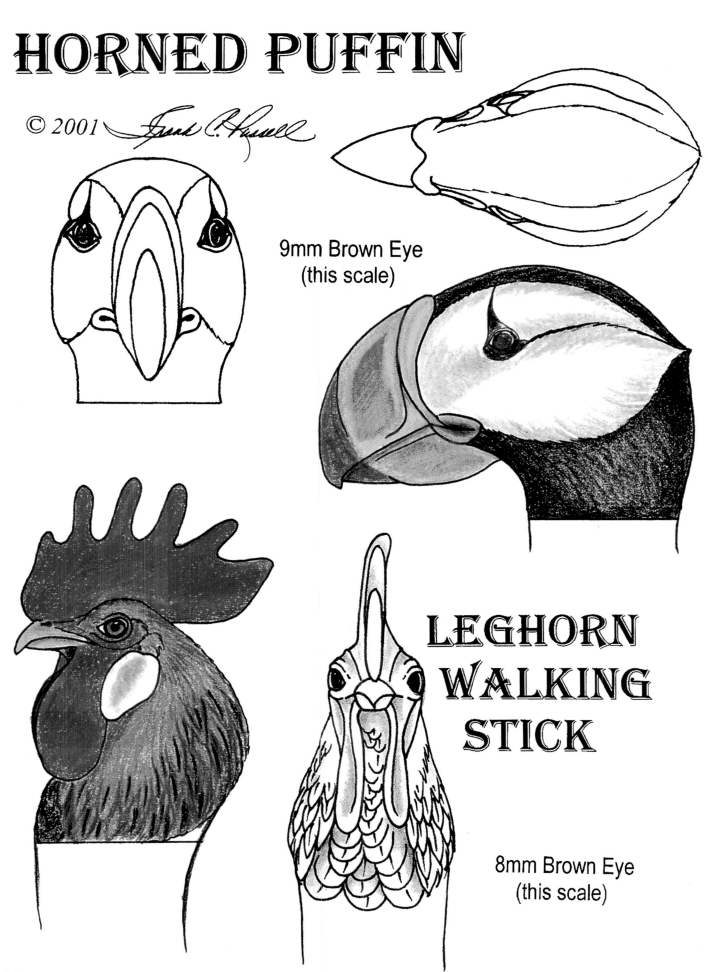

9mm Brown Eye
(this scale)

LEGHORN WALKING STICK

8mm Brown Eye
(this scale)

MALLARD CANE

© 2001 *Frank C. Russell*

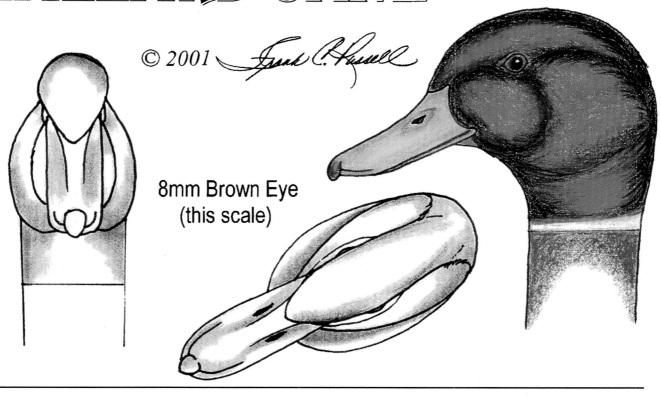

8mm Brown Eye
(this scale)

MALLARD WALKING STICK

© 2001 *Frank C. Russell*

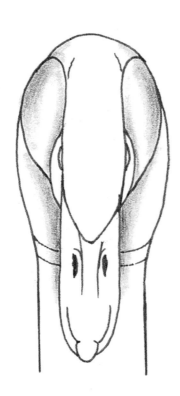

8mm Brown Eye
(this scale)

© 2001

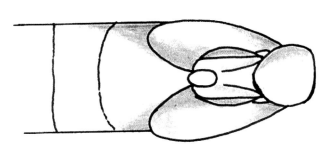

9mm Brown Eye
(this scale)

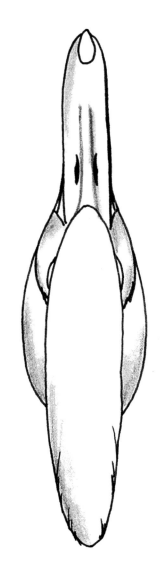

RING-NECKED PHEASANT

SANDHILL CRANE

7mm Brown Eye
(this scale)

9mm Brown Eye
(this scale)

© 2001

Under Beak Detail

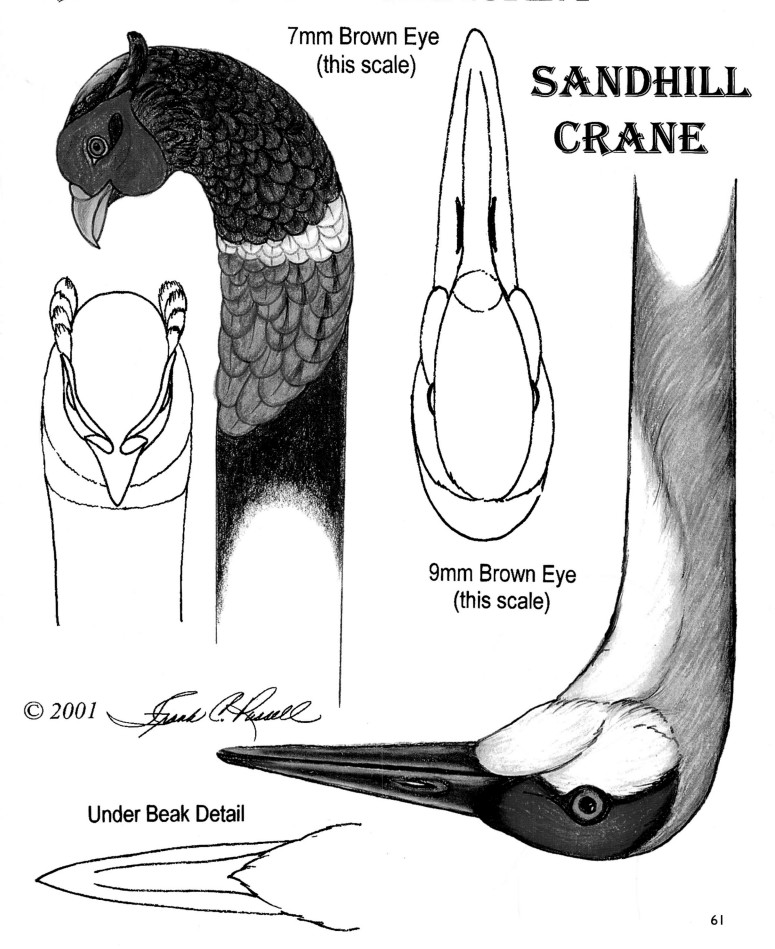

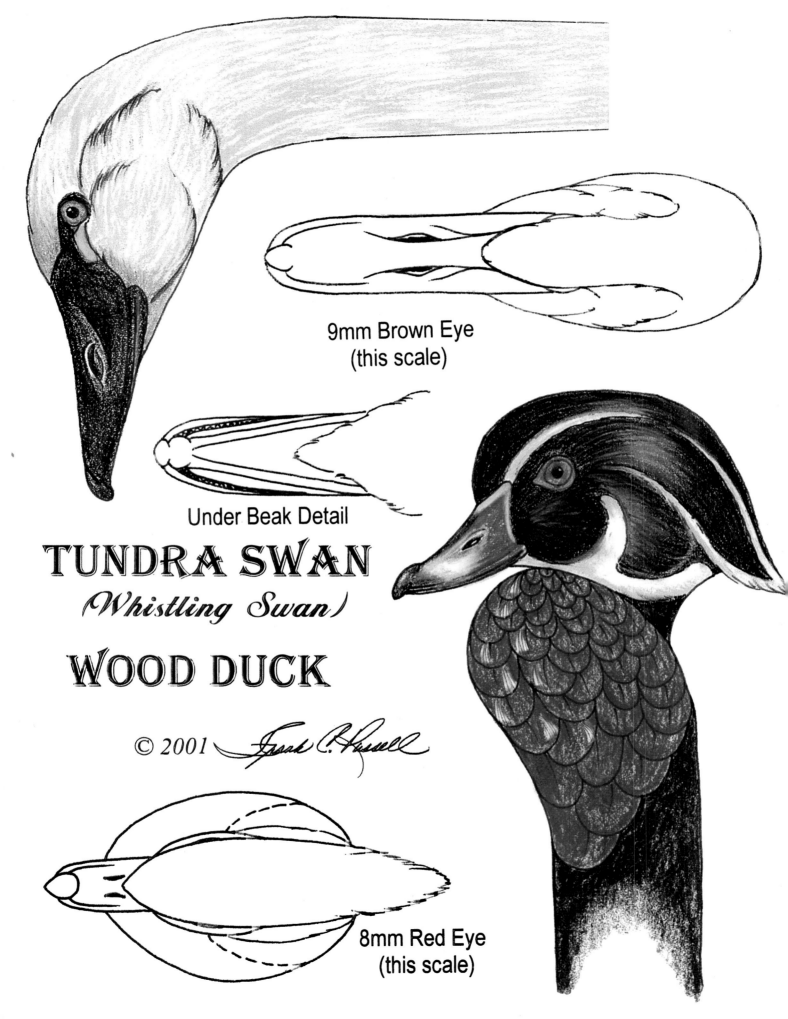

9mm Brown Eye
(this scale)

Under Beak Detail

TUNDRA SWAN
(Whistling Swan)

WOOD DUCK

© 2001 Frank C. Russell

8mm Red Eye
(this scale)

Cane and Stick Use

If you walk or hike through the forests and mountains as much as I do on my scouting trips, a walking stick is as necessary as good walking shoes. A walking stick is an assist to any journey afoot, whether it is through the woods or just a leisurely jaunt through the neighborhood.

If I'm not on a well beaten path, I find first that a stick helps me to keep my balance while trekking through forest growth, across hillsides, crossing brooks or waterways (especially beaver dams), ledges, and broken ground areas such as areas of gravel or shale. If I have had a particularly steep climb and want to rest, I cup both hands over the top of the stick and lean against it. It is sometimes better to rest in this manner than to remove my packsack and find a place to sit.

I find a walking stick very helpful in keeping errant dogs at a distance when I walk around the neighborhood where I winter in Florida. I never advance onto private property, but if the dog is loose and tries to attack or hinder my advance along the sidewalk, it runs an extremely high risk of receiving a thump on the head or the butt if it doesn't stop. It usually only takes one such encounter to ensure that, thereafter, I walk in peace. I have watched mailmen, and I wouldn't deliver mail unless high wages and a large stick were standard issue.

I have no idea how many times my walking sticks have prevented me from falling. They have saved me from falling while crossing fallen trees, stepping off curbs, stumbling onto a curb, slipping on wet leaves or frozen ground, or losing my balance on an incline. I once strained my back, and the doctor recommended that anytime I walked, until I had recovered, I should use either a cane that fit or a walking stick held at a comfortable level. I asked him how the stick would relieve my back and he said that not only would it relieve back strain, but also it would ease tension on hips, legs, knees, and feet.

A walking stick affords additional strength and balance by taking pressure off the back, hips, and to some extent the legs while going uphill, and eases shock to the shins and knees while going downhill (especially with a pack), often without the hiker/walker realizing it. I have a cousin who has hiked the entire length of the Appalachian Trail, along with many others. He has told me of times where he has waited out a heavy downpour by sitting under a ground cloth that was made into a "tent" by using the walking stick as a center pole and anchoring the corners with rocks and/or tying them to trees.

Sometimes I hike areas that I am not familiar, especially in the South. When I come to suspicious areas such as thick swampy areas that might house dangerous critters such as snakes, 'gators,

and the like, I poke my stick ahead and "feel" my way along the path. I wave my stick back and forth much as a blind man would use his white cane to sense his way along a sidewalk. In thick areas I will use the stick to open the way by pushing brush, palmettos, and other hanging growth out of the way.

Important aspects of any walking stick:

> it should fit;
> it should be light enough so as not to be burdensome.

Often I will meet folks on the trail who are dragging their walking sticks rather than using them as a trekking aid. Close inspection usually reveals a large stick that is not only heavy, but ill fitting:

> it must be rugged enough to support the user, whether bracing with it or leaning on it;
> it should be attractive (in the eye of the user ?).

Hand/Wrist Straps (and How to Use Them)

If you do serious walking or hiking then you will want to provide your walking stick with a wrist strap. If you add a strap, be sure that it is wide enough to give comfort and support to your wrist. Most manufactured walking or trekking sticks are provided with adjustable straps. These straps are usually made of one-inch nylon webbing. The webbing is twisted to allow an easy grip on the stick and to provide comfortable support to the wrist, which allows the forearm to work with comfort in conjunction with the arm, shoulder, and ultimately the back.

For my heavy use hiking sticks, I install a 1/2-inch strap of leather or nylon. Onto that strap I slide a sheep skin sleeve about three inches long. That sleeve rests on the bottom of the loop of the strap where it makes contact with the top my wrist.

The majority of casual walkers don't use straps, and many who do, believe that the strap is there primarily to keep them from dropping or losing their stick. However, if the stick and wrist strap are used properly, the holding hand shouldn't get tired.

The accepted way to position the hand within the strap is to:

1. Put the hand through the strap, starting between the stick and the loop of the strap.

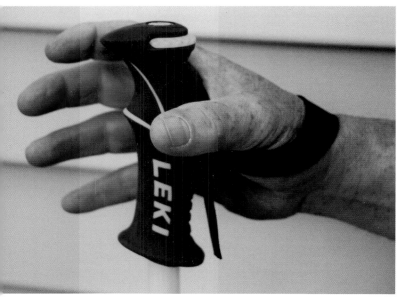

2. Bring the hand down on top of the strap, allowing the fingers to cradle the two sides of the strap and the walking stick.

3. If the strap has a buckle or tension adjustment through the handle, tighten snugly, but comfortably. *Do not* over-*tighten*.

4. Lightly grip the pole handle with two or three fingers and the thumb (don't grip too tightly because your hand and fingers will get unnecessarily tired and/or sore).

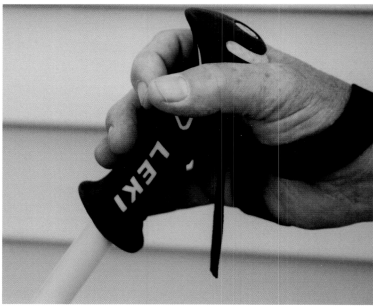

5. With your fingers, guide the pole to where you want to plant it, still very loosely holding it in your hand, then plant it on the ground with the weight of your body, pack, etc. transferring to the wrist strap via your wrist and arm.

Thanks to Smith Edwards of Stowe, Vermont, for modeling the above handgrip sequence.

Whether casually afoot for exercise with a walking stick, or hiking with two trekking sticks under a loaded backpack, any strain or tension associated with planting the stick(s) and the transference of any weight to and through them, should be on the wrists and arms, and not on the fingers and hands. Once you learn about, enjoy, and come to rely on the luxury of a wrist strap, you will probably find it uncomfortable to use a walking stick without one. If your stick has a wrist strap, it isn't necessary to grip the stick in the same manner that you would if it didn't have a strap. Keep your grip light enough so that you remove strain from your fingers and relieve that "white-knuckle" grip. Good Hiking!